Innocent Terrorist

Alam Ghafoor

New Age Publishers UK

INNOCENT TERRORIST

Copyright © Alam Ghafoor 2011

Published by New Age Publishers UK, 4th Floor, Media Factory, Kirkham Street, Preston, England, PR1 2HE.

www.newagepublishers.co.uk

ISBN 978-0-9570960-7-3

Innocent Terrorist

PREFACE

This book is a true story although some names have been changed to protect the identity of the individuals mentioned.

I wrote this book as a means of self-therapy to the traumatic experience that I went through.

The many friends and people that I met all asked me to go into detail of how one copes in extreme situations.

What did I do and what actions did I take?

I think it stands that although this was what I thought was an isolated case, I found out later that many others around the world have been through a similar situation.

We should be aware that sometimes things way beyond our control happen to us and around us.

Although the world has changed, the one thing that we always have control of is our internal response, our minds belong to us.

Many people have lost sight of that.

ACKNOWLEDGEMENTS

I dedicate this book to my dear mother who passed away in 2009. She was my rock and my greatest supporter. Always encouraging me and telling me to follow my dream and never let anything or anyone stand in my way. Her unwavering belief in me even when I doubted myself was solid. Seeing her become weak through illness and then her life ebb away as I held her hand was the toughest single thing in my life. Not a single day passes without her coming to mind and I often wish I could still seek her advice.

I also add my wonderful son Aqeel and of course my beautiful wife Menaz (and daughter Sana) who I met after mothers death.

She has taken over the mantle and is my yin. I thank her for her patience and support

I want to thank my brother Amar for his help and understanding. My friend Billy for keeping spirits high.

Big thanks to New Age Publishers.

To all my Mentors and teachers who taught me the skills and attitude that has helped me and shaped me.

My heartfelt gratitude for those I haven't named you know who you are.

INTRODUCTION

This book is written by myself. All viewpoints are my own.

There are times when I bring in the views of my friends who were in the same situation. The words and views are theirs.

I wanted you, the reader, to understand what I was experiencing and my thoughts and actions.

In some of the situations there was a crossover between us so to give you a feel of how we all act differently in a given situation I decided to include their accounts.

As you sit there and read ask yourself what would I do? How would I feel?

Chapter 1
Fried Chicken and Nylon Suits

Wednesday 20th July 2005 9 pm

It was a typical hot and balmy evening in Dubai. I had been here a couple of times before, but this was my first experience of the Emirates in July, which is considered the peak of summer. It's always scorching here; that goes without saying. But for the last few days, the temperature had been hitting the mid 40's during the day, sometimes even creeping up to 50 Celsius. That's a heat that just can't be described accurately enough. Saying 'hot' or 'baking' or whatever, just doesn't seem to do it justice somehow. One thing we soon learned was that the authorities never officially recognise it being quite that high, as 50 degrees is the point on the scale when the workers on the many construction sites are legally entitled to down tools and seek out some shade. There is no way the authorities would allow that. Nothing can halt the super-rich Sultanate's never-ending thirst for expansion and modernisation. Whether it is reclaiming land from the Arabian Sea, or reaching ever higher into the Heavens, the thirst has been unquenchable for the last two decades.

In the evening it cools down to a less oppressive mid to

high 20's, but then the humidity steps up a gear and gives you something new to complain about. You step out of the house freshly showered and within minutes you're sweating like you've just completed a workout at the local Gym. The air seems to bear down on you, thick and heavy, making every action, even one as simple as breathing, an unwelcome chore.

"Let's do something different for a change. How about we go to the cinema? I hear there is a new Bollywood blockbuster showing," Z said all excited.

"No, it's too hot in there; the air-con is useless. Let's just chill out at the Seashells, ok?" Raf shot down his friends suggestion a little too tersely, I thought.

"Well I'm hungry," I said diplomatically. "Let's eat first then we can decide."

Without the need for discussion we headed off to the KFC restaurant in Al-Karama.

Al-Karama or simply Karama is a residential district of Dubai and is part of the bustling older city. It's known in Dubai as a centre for cheap furniture and covert counterfeit branded goods i.e. watches and handbags. It also boasts a huge variety of good and affordable restaurants, authentic cuisines from India, Pakistan, Philippines, Sri Lanka, China, Singapore, Thailand and of course Arabic. With so much fantastic choice we opted for KFC.

We'd gotten into the unhealthy habit of grabbing a family sized bucket - half normal, half spicy - almost on a daily basis. Our bulging waistlines and ever-slowing pace were testament to our bad diet. Those buckets should come with a warning as I am sure they have a secret ingredient that is seriously addictive. The discussion veered from the usual subjects of friends over here, to friends in the UK. Somebody we all knew had been dumped by their girlfriend and somebody had been caught with his pants down by the missus. Somebody had struck gold with a deal and somebody else had lost their shirt. We laughed, we joked, we talked about the same old things and we ate our fried chicken. There were only the three of us; Raf, Z and myself. Faz had already phoned saying he was held up, but would meet up with us later on in the evening.

We finished our feast and decided to go to another of our regular haunts, the Seashells Hotel. This was just round the corner from Karama, located near the gold souk and what they call Computer Street where there are dozens of electrical stores and computer shops.

Inside the lobby of the Hotel and to the immediate left as you enter there is a little Indian restaurant called Dawaat which translates as invitation to feast. You leave the brightly lit lobby and are immediately plunged into near blackness as you step through the doors into the dimness beyond. As your eyes slowly adjust to the darkness they are drawn to the stage area which pulsates with a rack of flashing coloured lights. The décor, if you look closely, is very grubby and run-down. Thankfully the décor is pretty low down on the list of reasons why we come here so often. The place is nothing special; the food is quite good providing you order the right dish. Whatever you do don't order the soup or you will likely be shitting through the eye of a needle all night and probably throughout the next day. There speaks the voice of experience and it was an experience I plan on avoiding in the future. But the menu is not the reason we are drawn here like moths to a flame. We come for the nightly entertainment, or the 'Indian Cabaret' as it is not entirely accurately billed. There is always a decent band on stage, along with a dancing troupe of girls that represent a varied cross section of Asia; Indian, Nepalese, Bangladeshi and even Pakistani girls sometimes. The girls wear heavy make-up; a disguise so good that all of them looked anywhere from beautiful to stunning. If you saw them in the day minus the make up most of them would frighten the shit out of you. I know this because some friends had managed to secure daytime dates with a couple of the girls and had received the fright of their lives when they had turned up.

"My God, she looked like my Grandmother in the cold light of day!" Mubeen had chuckled.

But here in the restaurant, they were stars on a carefully lit stage, wallowing in the adoration of their audience. There were couples and even whole families present at times, but mainly it was just men in groups of two or more; all trying desperately to catch the eye of their very own Ashwary Rai lookalike. (former Miss India now a Bollywood starlet)

During the dancing routines, those who wanted to attract the girls' attention would throw plain cards at the stage. These are plain white business sized cards with nothing printed on them and the guys throwing are not allowed to write numbers or any details on them. The cards are valued at something like around 6 or 7 dirhams per card (around 1 pound sterling) and can only be bought in batches of 1000 at a time. I am sure if you had regular patronage you could have the price reduced to around 4or 5 dirhams per card but I would say that if you have given out a thousand cards with no success then it is time to rethink your dating strategy. I had been told one guy had spent over 50 grand over several weeks before he finally got the number of the girl he liked!

But the cards symbolised more than just money. Sometimes hundreds of cards would be thrown at once, supposedly to show appreciation for a particular girl or even the singer if he or she hit a difficult high note. In reality tens of thousands of dirhams were wasted and all just for a quick sideways glance and a smile if you were lucky. Some guys went crazy and spent every night here imagining themselves becoming lovers or, even better, marrying one of the stars up on the stage. I heard it said that the record for one night was around 100,000 pounds sterling. Luckily there was no obligation to throw and we had never thrown a single card between us.

There were also a couple of boy dancers. I say boys but they were probably around 19 or 20 years of age. They were malnourished and pasty looking, which is ironic considering sunlight is one thing that Dubai is never lacking. And then there were two older men who were the professional singers, complete with seventies haircuts and cheap nylon suits; the sort that rub and give off static when you walk. These boys really were legends in their own mind. They seemed immensely proud of their vocal skills, often giving each other complementary sideways glances after hitting a particularly high note. Either that or there was – as we all suspected - more to their friendship than just singing duets.

Collectively, the two singers, the girl dancers and the young boys mimed and danced and occasionally sang along to Bollywood songs; some pop, some classical. Dubai has hundreds of places like this that put on a show every night of the week. We didn't like to stay at home indoors, sweltering in the heat, so these places gave us somewhere cool and pleasant to hang out.

Some places are better presented than others and some places always seem to have prettier girls than their competition. We found to our horror, after stumbling into a particularly rough-looking joint, that some places have really rough looking performers to match the equally rough clientele! We only made the one stop there and it was quite a short one, if I remember correctly.

So we always seemed to gravitate back to the Seashell. Like an old and comfortable pair of shabby shoes that we slipped into and felt at home. Everybody knew us. The waiters, the managers, door staff; all of them would come running up to greet us as soon as we entered, hoping for a good tip at the end of the night. Or, as Z once said,

"Just as likely they are after a connection with somebody who could get them a visa to England, Europe or America."

Although back home in their respective countries it would be considered good fortune to be working in Dubai, anyone who had worked the low-paid menial jobs there soon realised that life wasn't really that great and the real yellow brick road was still to the west.

We had friends who we would regularly meet there and many others who would drop by sometime in the evening as they did the circuit. This was what we called visiting as many of our favourite venues as possible in a single night, similar to a pub crawl, but generally without the imbibing of alcohol. I say generally, because alcohol, like most things in life, is freely available if you have the right money and some of our friends would occasionally partake.

So life was good. It was very much a home away from home and we felt extremely comfortable here. There were a few negatives, such as the T.V which is diabolical.

Repeat after repeat of American and British series, or their poor Middle Eastern copies of such. Some of the channels pump out movies all day long, all very heavily censored and barely worth watching.

Having sat there for a couple of hours, we realised that we probably wouldn't be seeing Faz tonight as it was past his curfew. He had to be home by a certain time because:

1. The missus insisted on it and we knew who wore the trousers.

2. He had work in the morning and the drive from Sharjah to Dubai was not an easy one. There is only one big road leading in and out and everybody and their camel makes use of it. The traffic jams are legendary.

So we got some drinks in and settled down to watch the girls.

"So you don't think to order me a drink?" said a familiar voice.

"Hey, Faz ! We thought we wouldn't see you tonight. Thought maybe the leash was a little tight this late at night, my friend," Raf joked.

Faz sat down and the group was complete.

"I heard the pretty girl with the big almond eyes will be dancing alone tonight," Faz ventured.

"Ahh, so now we know," said Z with a smile. "A wife at home and still he lusts after the sweet young girls, eh?"

"No, no, it's not like that, Z. I just appreciate beauty, in the same way I like to look at the beautiful paintings in the Gallery." Faz said seriously.

"I am just teasing you Faz; don't take offence, dude."

We sat in silence for a few minutes, just taking in the show, when Faz turned back to Z and said with a smile,

"But she is bloody beautiful though!"

Raf's phone rang. His concentration on the dancers

broken, he walked off briskly towards the hotel lobby, where the music was not so loud. Plus he probably didn't want anybody to get the wrong idea of the kinds of places he was hanging out in.

Z's phone vibrated on the curry -stained tablecloth, he picked it up, looked at the screen and took a walk too.

****

Z: The phone call

I walked outside to take a call. I didn't recognise the number and thought about ignoring it and getting back to the cabaret. But the ringing was somehow insistent, so curiosity got the better of me.

"Hello? Who is this?" I asked cautiously.

It turned out to be a local Arab claiming to be a taxi driver. He said he had a woman in his cab who had asked him to call me and find out where I was, so that she could come and meet me. I was puzzled to say the least.

"Who is she? What's her name?" I asked, quite reasonably.

"I don't know sir, she speaks very little English. She just wants to know where you are."

I knew for sure that I hadn't given my number out to anybody, least of all a woman who couldn't speak English.

"I am sorry, but you must have the wrong number. I have no idea who this woman is. And anyway, I'm happily married with children." I said, hanging up and terminating the call.

I stared at the phone in my hand, mulling over the strange call, when the screen illuminated once more, flashing up the same number as before. I flipped the clamshell angrily.

"Look, I have already told you that you have a wrong number. Try someone else!"

"Please sir; she is very insistent that this is the number I should call. She won't get out of my cab until I take her to you," the taxi driver said pleadingly.

So I asked him which number he was supposed to be ringing and sure enough, he repeated my number back to me.

"Please sir, just let me bring her to you. If there is some mix-up, she will surely accept that she has written the number down incorrectly and I can get her out of my car."

"Where are you now" I asked.

"I am just outside Karama, sir."

Against my better judgement I told him I was in the Dawaat restaurant at the Seashells Hotel. He thanked me and said he would be there in no more than ten minutes. I waited outside the hotel looking around for a taxi to turn up. Three or four vehicles pulled into the large sweeping driveway that branched off the main road and led directly to the front of the hotel, so the valet parking guys could earn their money.

I casually noticed there were two guys in the first car and two in the second, but couldn't really see into the third. All were big, thickset men of Arab descent, something you tend to notice when you've been in Dubai long enough. The Arabs never look comfortable when dressed in anything other than a traditional dish dash, so they tend to stick out like sore thumbs. Still, looking around I didn't think anything of it until I watched them exit their vehicles and walk straight for me. The lead guy, probably the one in charge, asked for my I.D. card. It was a strange thing to ask outright – no small talk and no explanation - but I told him the truth, which was that it was in my car. The biggest man, standing to the side of the leader, reached forward and grabbed my phone off me, telling me that they also wanted to speak to my friends. They surrounded me and almost frog-marched me back inside the Hotel and into the restaurant.....

****

<u>Raf</u>

My phone went off, so I took a walk into the lobby to answer it. A cousin of mine back in the UK had decided to ring and have a chat. I was half listening to them, while texting on my other phone. I knew that once my cousin got started, I would have my ear chewed for a while, so I sat down on the oversized lobby sofa, with the air conditioning blowing directly on me. I could see that Z had followed me out of the restaurant a minute or so later. He carried on walking past me and went and stood outside just in front of the hotel, pacing around talking animatedly into his phone.

I finished my texting and was still listening to my cousin chat away about nothing important. I looked up and saw Z come back into the lobby accompanied by a group of Arab men, who I assumed must be friends of his. He walked straight past without acknowledging me and went back into Dawaat to re-join Alam and Faz.

****

Alam

Faz and I were talking about his work situation. He had been making plans to break out on his own, having worked at the same place for a number of years. He was tired of seeing younger guys coming in and starting on similar wages to him and quickly progressing up the corporate ladder, or worse; people coming in from Europe or the UK on a higher level than him who knew little about the job. All of them would regularly come to him for advice, but they would get rewarded for doing a great job, while his role was continually overlooked.

This was not an uncommon problem in Dubai. Somebody from the Asian continent with similar qualifications and expertise to someone from the West will be paid half of the salary as the Western worker, as well as being offered a far more inferior benefits package. I sympathised with my friend, who smiled and made a 'but what can you do' gesture with his hands. I sensed movement out of the corner of my eye and looked up to see Z walking back into the restaurant with an unknown group of men. Two of them were big ugly brutes, the rest were smaller sized, but ugly none the less. All the guys with Z were casually dressed, although the fashions were a little outdated. As the group came nearer, a stage-light washed over them and I could see the look on Z's face was not a happy one. When they got to our table, the big brute who had led the mini procession immediately grabbed me by the shoulders and dragged me up and out of the chair.

"Gentleman," said the obvious leader, "we would like you to accompany us outside. Please don't make a scene. There is no need for any unpleasantness."

The words had been spoken in a soft and unthreatening manner, but the underlying warning was crystal clear. Faz got up and followed obediently like he was told to. As we all walked through the restaurant, everybody just froze. The waiters, the dancers, the customers; all eyes followed us to the door. A weird feeling I can't describe came over me, quickly replaced by an overpowering sense of fear.

Once in the lobby we were unceremoniously pushed down onto the sofa.

"Sit down there and be quiet," the leader said. "Hand over your mobile phones, keys and anything else you have in your pockets."

The four of us huddled together awkwardly on the three-seater sofa. The suits stood over us, blocking any chance for us to get away.

"What's going on?" I asked. A quite reasonable request, I thought.

"Be quiet," the guy directly in front of me muttered menacingly. "Keep your mouth shut and there will be no problems."

An Arab in full dish dash suddenly appeared behind our watchers. He was whispering into an earpiece that looked like one of the cheap ones you get for free with a mobile phone. I was confused and remember thinking just what the hell is happening here.

Again I spoke up. "What's happening? What's going on?"

The big bastard in front of me leaned forward and almost whispered,

"I've told you already to keep quiet. Don't make me tell you a third time."

I sat back as best I could and tried to calm myself. 'What the hell is happening here' I repeated to myself. I realised my breath was shallow and stuttering, so I consciously took in several slow, deep breaths. In through the nose, out through the mouth, in through the nose, out.......

I realised the leader had walked to the front of the Hotel and was looking around impatiently like he was waiting for someone. Then suddenly he turned back towards us and made a hand gesture to one of the suits. Z and I were grabbed and quickly marched outside as a car pulled up. The lead goon pulled the back door open and we were thrown roughly into the back of it. The driver spun round and cuffed Z, the front passenger cuffed me.

My heart was going ten to the dozen. The adrenalin was surging through my veins creating a nauseous light-headed feeling. What are the options? Fight or flight? There wasn't much of a chance to do either, now we were handcuffed in the back of their car. Why did we conform so easily in the restaurant? Why didn't we just fight them off? It was four on six; not good odds, but not impossible! My mind continued racing, a hundred thoughts bombarding it all at once. Shit-scared one second, worrying that I'm going to be sick over my captive, then alternatively thinking maybe one of our friends is playing a joke and just wants to see how scared we are. Maybe it's that fucker Jeremy Beadle? Sure he retired a few years ago, maybe this is his comeback? Or are we being kidnapped? For what purpose; a ransom? Don't make me laugh, I don't have fuck all to my name. Shit, there must be hundreds, probably thousands of people who are richer than me here in Dubai. Maybe Raf secretly is an heir or something. Or Z ? Yeah, Z is more likely. That's probably what it is, it's him they want.

This was the way my mind was thinking. Irrational.

Illogical. Shit-scared. The adrenaline eventually took a dump and I slumped back in my seat, suddenly exhausted. A strange calmness descended and my brain started functioning properly. The very first thing that screamed out in that small window of clarity was: This can't be happening here! Dubai has zero crime! The streets are safe to walk at any time, regardless of whether you're male or female. If this is a kidnap, surely they wouldn't do it in full view of a restaurant full of people? Somebody who witnessed it will be on the phone to the Police as soon as we left, wouldn't they? My fear was once again replaced with confusion. I asked yet again,

"What's going on?"

The same reply as before. "Be quiet."

The guy in the front of me turned round and a gun suddenly appeared through the gap between the front seats and was waved menacingly back and forth at us. I couldn't hear anything but the sound of my heart beating faster and harder in my ears. My head started spinning so fast that the feeling of nausea returned with a vengeance and I desperately fought the urge to vomit. When you live in the Middle East, you hear all the stories about kidnaps and the like, but it usually happens in places like Iran, Iraq or Beirut. Not here. No way.

Fuck. Are we about to be killed in cold blood? If this was a joke it had gone too fucking far. The car tore off at a crazy speed, all spinning tyres and the smell of rubber. The guy drove like a maniac, as if we had just robbed a bank and were being chased by the cops. As we careered round corners with the tyres screeching their disapproval, the front passenger still had his gun pointed towards us in the back. In fact it was more pointed towards me than Z. I remembered that film 'Pulp Fiction' where the black guy sitting in the back of the car, has his head blown off by Travolta, accidentally pulling the trigger when they drive over a pothole. This seemed the exact same scenario and I just stared down the barrel; waiting for it to go off.

Funny the shit that goes through your mind at the strangest of times. I sat there, remembering when my father had a heart attack and I had gone to the hospital with him in the ambulance. I had to crouch on the floor of the Accident and Emergency Room while the nurses buzzed all around him. From my low vantage point I was the right height to glimpse the black stockings as the nurses hurried back and forth. That, coupled with the uniform itself, I couldn't keep my eyes off those legs…phew!!!

The car swung hard around a corner, bringing me out of my daydream. Ordinarily I would have smiled at such a memory, but at that moment I think I had forgotten how to. Brought back to my harsh reality, I realised we were driving even faster now and more erratically. Maybe somebody at the restaurant had phoned the Police and now we were being chased? But it wasn't to be. The car pulled sharply to the right, into a deserted car park. My legs started shaking uncontrollably and I was hyperventilating. I would like to tell you how Z was at this point, but to be honest; I was in my own little world, completely unaware of my friend. The brakes were slammed on sharply and the car slid to a sharp halt, rocking gently on its shocks. The front passenger jumped out leaving the door open and started talking excitedly on his phone. I looked out my window, turned awkwardly around, straining to look behind me through the rear screen, hoping to see the cavalry coming to save us. The Police were nowhere to be seen. No sirens. No flashing lights in the distance. Not a fucking peep.

All I could see was a normal car driving along the same road we had just been on. It came to the car park entrance and pulled sharply in. Plain clothes maybe ? Detectives ? Over here! It headed straight for us and pulled up just behind our car. I could hear a muffled conversation ensue, but I couldn't make anything out as I don't speak Arabic. What I could hear though, was the boot being opened, someone rummaging inside and something being taken out. The boot slammed shut and the men had another conversation. A door opened and then closed and the car behind turned over its ignition and sped away.

"No! No! Where are you going!" I screamed inside my head. A couple of minutes later, our passenger opened my door. He leant in and gave me a weird smile. Almost sympathetic. I think I smiled back. Maybe the guy in the other car was in charge and had told our goon that he had the wrong guys? I raised my cuffed hands with a shrug, as if to say, "are you going to take these off me now?" The man leaned in to the car and pulled a hood roughly over my head.

I sat in silence. Probably in shock. I heard the other rear door open and knew Z was getting the same treatment. He too, said nothing. The car started up and we sped off again. Once again my mind swam with a miasma of black thoughts. The bastards are going to shoot us. We haven't done anything wrong or upset anyone, why are they doing this? Maybe they know they have the wrong guys, so they have got to cover their tracks. That's why they can't face us.

I thought I heard Z quietly sobbing and decided enough is enough. Am I going to just sit here obediently and wait for a bullet in the head? I have to do something. I exaggerated my hyperventilating.

"I can't breathe," I half gasped. "Take it off me," I said between exaggerated wheezes. Surely they would have to take the hood off. If I could get them to stop the car it might buy us some time. Somebody might see us and raise the alarm, or we may be able to make a run for it? Oh, shit. They won't take Z's hood off though. It didn't matter anyway. They turned on the radio and ignored me.

A sharp turn and we pulled in to a side road or maybe a dirt-track, because the ride became very bumpy. We bounced around on the back seats, banging knees and elbows into each other. I thought we were driving deep into the desert where they would shoot us and bury our bodies where they would never be found.

The car stopped abruptly again, sliding along and kicking up stones. I thought, 'Doesn't this bastard know how to apply the brakes properly?' Doors were opened and somebody grabbed me in a very rough manner and half-dragged, half-pulled me out into the hot night air. The contrast of the cold air conditioning in the car and the hot air outside was too much for me and my stomach flipped, making me feel like I was about to throw up. I started gagging but nobody was paying any attention.

I felt two people take an arm each, force me upright and start dragging me away from the vehicle. I soon stumbled over something and realised it was some steps.

"Walk! Keep walking," the guy on my left said. It was pretty poor English and heavily accented, but I understood it anyway. I stumbled up a couple more steps and felt the air conditioning hit me.

"Alam! Alam! Are you there?"

I heard Z calling out and realised he must still be by

the car. So I was alone now. I was dragged further into the building and I heard voices coming at me from all directions; some clearly very excited by my arrival. I felt the ground change suddenly from a tiled floor to one that was thickly carpeted. I was forced into a chair and a door slammed shut behind me. An eerie silence descended. I wondered if everyone had left the room? All I could hear was my heart pounding like a kettle drum and I was conscious that my breathing was kind of shallow and stuttering. I took a few deep breaths and tried my best to relax .....

****

I had known Raf for a little over two years. We had been introduced by a mutual friend of ours called Bash. I was at college with Bash way back in the late eighties and we had met when I was asked to give a talk to those interested in studying law. Now this only happened because I had been unlucky enough to be picked for jury service at the local crown court and the tutor somehow thought this qualified me to give a talk on my experience. Anyway, long story short, Bash and I just clicked – maybe my southern accent made him gravitate to me – and we developed a firm friendship that lasted for years, even during the times when he was away at university and we could only get together on too few occasions. After he had graduated and was working in different parts of the country, whenever he was in the area he would call and we would meet, catch up on the news and discuss our plans to make our first million.

Around the spring of 2003 having learnt his trade and gained the necessary experience, Bash opened an office in

Dewsbury, Yorkshire. The day he signed the lease on the office, he called me over and we started discussing the overseas real estate opportunities in places like the USA and Dubai. It was during this particular meeting that Bash suggested that I meet a couple of friends and business partners of his.

So this is when I met Raf. He appeared to be a shy, quiet type who didn't ask too many questions. He is probably around 5' 11" with a medium build, although he told me that he used to weigh over 18 stone. He had a wheatish-brown complexion, had lost most of the hair from the top of his head and wore glasses. He has a friendly face that somehow makes you know straight off that he is a decent guy. He is married with three kids, but from the look in his eyes when he talks about married life, I have always suspected that things are not too rosy in that department.

After a few friendly meet ups, we all got down to some serious discussions about what we were going to do about the opportunities we knew existed out there in the big wide world.

It was me and Raf that undertook most of the early legwork for the business. We developed a good friendship travelling together to China and the USA. Like I said, Raf is quiet, but very hard working. He seemed to be at it day and night; his phone ringing non-stop with different tones for his various businesses. I soon learned he is determined to be successful and committed to bettering himself. When there is a chance to relax for an evening, nothing gives Raf more pleasure than taking in an Indian film followed by some good old fashioned Indian home cooking. Our friendship became stronger the more we travelled and the more time we spent together. Raf is a couple of years older than me, so I looked upon him as an older brother. There were times when he would fly off the handle and really flip out, but just as quickly he would calm down. As I got to know him over time he would confide in me little things which gave me a better understanding of his character, such as the most common reason for losing his temper. Some of the workers he employed in his many businesses took advantage of his good nature and were a bunch of lazy bastards. This angered me too, as I knew this guy would go out of his way to help almost anybody, even if it inconvenienced him. But I guess, as much as Raf can't help his generous nature, the lazy bastards can't help theirs.

The introduction to Z was brought about by a happy accident; Bash had arranged dinner with friends, who just happened to bring him along. I was seated next to him and so we spent most of the evening talking together. He was just 5 feet 2 and built like a wrestler with his Buddha belly and massive arms. He was a funny, sarcastic, fast talking guy who had been married for over twenty years. He had probably developed this way of talking because he had seven kids and it was the only way he would be heard in his house! Z had lived in London all his life and had spent many years working for central government, before branching out and developing an extensive property portfolio that included a chain of retirement homes. A member of Mensa, (his claim) well educated and articulate, I knew straight off that I liked this guy and this was the start of a true friendship. As I got to know him over the next few months, my hunch proved to be right, as we clicked due to the same mentality and sense of humour. One thing we don't share to the same degree is Z's love of shopping. I say shopping, but specifically it's all about shoes. I'm not sure whether Z has a foot fetish, but either way, I figure he must have a bigger collection of shoes than Imelda Marcos; every time we went shopping he would buy at least one pair, sometimes even two.

Bash, Raf and myself visited Dubai in February 2005; it was the first visit there for myself and Raf, but Bash had previous visits notched up. Several friends of his had migrated to Dubai over the years and they had offered to help and guide us in our search for property bargains. It was only a short visit of about 5 days, but I was impressed by how alive with activity the whole place was, with massive skyscrapers being erected everywhere. I also thought just how well developed the infrastructure was and the ease with which we could find our way around. It wasn't really what I would call my impression of a desert oasis, but it was pretty damn close.

One of Ash's friends in Dubai was Faz; a Pakistani citizen who had been resident in Sharjah on and off for 13 years. They had met through friends on one of Ash's trips a few years previously and had kept in touch since then. On subsequent visits to Dubai, they would meet up and spend a lot of time together. In fact, I suspect it was Faz who had first taken Bash to Dawaat for the Cabaret, for when Bash suggested one night that we should go see some dancers, he spoke quietly to the taxi driver, who drove us straight there and Faz joined us later in the evening. Faz had years of experience working as an IT specialist and although generally he was content with his life in the Sultanate, he felt he was underpaid and undervalued. But he was happy with life overall and was happily married with two sons and a daughter. His accent was a mix of Middle Eastern with a hint of Indian-

English. He was a fun guy, at times joining in with the lads and joking around. But he could be a little moody over the most minor of things, like the time we ribbed him over the funky shirt he wore out one night. He was a tall pudgy-faced man with a definite Arabian look about him. He always slicked back his thinning hair with copious amounts of brylcreem and was generally always clean shaven and well groomed.

So my first impressions of Dubai had been great. I had met some good people, had some good times and even done some work, researching some investment opportunities. A couple of months later, after returning home, Faz rang out of the blue.

"Hey, Alam. It's Faz. How are you?"

"Hi Faz, yeah, still working hard, trying for that big one! You know how it is. How are you, my friend. Just a social call?" I asked.

"Well, yes and no. I wondered if you had plans to return here any time soon. You see, a friend has managed to get VIP passes to the Dubai World Cup next month. I don't know how much you know about it, but it is something not to be missed!" Faz said excitedly.

"So you are offering them to me?"

"Yes, to all my British friends. You, Bash, Raf and Z must all come if it is possible."

"Sounds good, Faz. Thank you for thinking of us. I'll have a chat with the gang and get back to you very soon. Is that ok?" I asked.

"Sure, my friend. Just don't take more than a day or two. These tickets might start burning a hole in my pocket. They are very special."

I thanked Faz and said my goodbyes. When I met up with the guys the next day and passed on the message, there was a silence for a few moments. I looked from face to face, waiting for some sort of reaction, either good or bad. Z broke out in a wide smile and looked at Raf who reciprocated. They both stood up and hugged each other, almost jumping up and down.

"The World Cup?" said Z. "I don't believe it. Do you know how prestigious it is?"

"It is a horse race, yes?" I said meekly.

"A horse race! A horse race he says!" Raf almost shouted. "Only the biggest, richest, most special event in the Middle East, my friend. Sultans and Kings and Presidents. You name it, they will be there. And all in the VIP! With us!"

I joined in the reverie, thinking that if this is how my friends react, well it has to be a good thing. The only one not jumping around with us was Bash.

"Bash. What is it? You are not excited?" Z asked him.

"I am sorry my friends. I can't go."

"What do you mean? What could possibly be more important? If it's business, then we will work while we are there."

"No, it's not that. It is a family commitment. I can't miss it," Bash said sadly. "You guys go; I know what a big deal the Cup is and I won't be responsible for you missing it."

"Thank you, Bash. You are a good friend," I replied sympathetically.

"Yes, Bash. I am sorry you can't be there," said Raf.

"But we will make sure we have a good time anyway!" Z added with a smile.

As luck would have it - if luck is the right word - one of Bash's family fell ill soon after and the family engagement was postponed. We phoned Faz in the hope that he still had a ticket and thankfully our good friend came up trumps. So we all returned to Dubai a few weeks later, in time for the World Cup. The event had been dreamed up by the Sheik to showcase his finest horses and pit them against the best in the world. The Cup drew in the richest and most powerful people from all over the world and allowed the Sheik to not only to showcase his horses, but also the wonder of Dubai itself. The Sheiks had set out to make this place a future model for how cities should be and they were certainly setting a high standard. All the menial jobs were taken by workers from the Indian subcontinent and everywhere you went people scurried to and fro on their way to clean something, build something, or serve someone. The sheer volume of traffic was surprising considering the relatively small size of the place; and the percentage of high-end models like Rolls Royce, Mercedes and BMW was probably higher than anywhere on earth. My favourite thing about Dubai overall, was the service at the 5 star hotels. They really lived up to their names with impeccable service that catered for every whim.

We met up with Faz on the morning of the Cup, all dressed up in our best suits for the occasion. The football stars and celebrities were already mixing and mingling; I spotted a few faces I recognised, but couldn't recall the names; unlike Bash, who sported a stupid grin and bounded around like an excited puppy, just because we were within touching distance of them. We took a slow walk through the VIP section, with Bash pointing out the people he recognised, but without plucking up the courage to approach anyone. Despite being fully entitled to be there, it still somehow felt like we were interlopers.

"Come on, let's go and actually see some racing," I

said. "We'll probably have more fun away from these people.

"I think so too," Faz agreed. I'm glad I'm not the only one who feels a little uncomfortable here."

Bash looked a little sad, but agreed anyway. So we all took a walk over to the racecourse and stood around waiting for the races to begin.

"Ah, so you have chosen your spot already, Gentlemen?" said a voice behind us.

I turned to see a small Indian man sweeping up just behind us.

"Yes, I think we'll have a good view here when the racing starts. Thank you."

"Best you get yourselves some food and beverages then Sir. It will be hours yet before any horses are out on the track."

The old man shuffled off and we just stood there smiling.

"No wonder we found such a good spot! We must look like idiots, standing here all alone." Faz said.

"Don't worry, we probably look like we're above all the 'see and be seen' nonsense," chuckled Bash. "Just smile and look cool and everyone will think we've done this a thousand times and are just bored by it all."

At this event we saw the two faces of Dubai, with its huge extremes of rich and poor. In the VIP section, surrounded by the super-rich, it was easy to overlook the huge army of poorly paid immigrants who made sure events such as these ran smoothly. As waiters and helpers ran back and forth serving their masters, we got the occasional glimpse of the workers slaving away in the back of the marquees. They were probably earning less that day than the price of one glass of champagne.

East meets West in the Sultanate and mix so well that the edges blur and blend and not just at special events such as the Horse racing. It was kind of surreal to see a mass of Muslims heading to the prayer area, while less than 50 yards away in the VIP tent, everyone knew that the alcohol flowed freely. Along with alcohol, gambling is not allowed in any of the Emirates, yet all the sheiks and many rich Arabs are avid gamblers. They get around the strict law by having their gambling accounts overseas and as you walked around you couldn't help but overhear them on their mobiles placing bets worth millions of pounds.

All around us were a sea of immaculately dressed Arab men, all seemingly with fat bellies popping through their flowing robes, stroking their fat faces with the assured confidence that only serious money brings. Most were talking excitedly to the well-manicured and expensively dressed women, paying particular attention to the blondes, desperately trying to impress them all. I could almost see the dollar signs in the women's eyes, along with the hope that they were laughing in the right places to all the tawdry and flirtatious talk aimed at them. Secretly hoping that maybe, just maybe the guy would fall in love with them, shower them with jewels and money and they would live forever in golden palaces, never wanting for anything again. While we were in Dubai, it seemed like everyone knew someone, who knew someone, who met a Sheik and struck lucky, either becoming a wife or a mistress.

I must assume that this kind of event was a more acceptable place to meet women than the so-called nightclubs that were dotted around the city. Everyone knew that they were owned by the Sheiks themselves and everyone also knew that they were nothing more than a cover. Step inside any of the more exclusive clubs and you soon realised it was really just a whore house; most were like meat markets packed to the rafters with girls from all over the world. In some of the clubs it was like a short trip around the globe. In one area you have Chinese corner, then Filipino street, then Romania avenue followed by Kazakhstan, Ukraine, Moscow then it's onto the African safari, with Somalia, Kenya, Ethiopia, Ghana. The Congo etc. The list goes on. The Arabs themselves have a voracious appetite for western looking women and in particular, good looking girls with blond hair and blue eyes always get top marks and top dollar.

Whenever I saw one or two of the girls leaving with a group of obviously well-connected men, I couldn't help but think back to a story I'd heard from a friendly club security guard we had all got chatting to. He told us that two girls from Turkmenistan had recently been picked up in the club and had not returned by the next evening. A few days later a bin bag was left in the car park next to the club and when one of the guard's colleagues had opened it, he found the dismembered bodies of the two girls. Video footage had shown that the car that took the girls bore the red registration plate of Saudi Arabia. As far as our security guard friend knew, the Police had not been to the club to question anyone and nobody was ever charged with the crime.

Incidents like this took place more often than you would think and always they were pretty much covered up to protect any Arab nationals that were involved. Everyone knows that cleaners, nannies and home helps from the Indian subcontinent and Philippines are routinely abused and raped and then just happen to 'accidentally' fall out of windows. If they dared to report the crime they themselves would most likely be jailed and would be flogged and beaten on a daily basis. To add insult, after the sentence is completed they would be deported from Dubai, with no money for the work they had done and no chance of ever returning.

So that was two examples of the law in Dubai and how it is applied. For the Arab nationals, some tourists and well-connected foreign residents there are one set of rules. This paints a pretty picture and keeps the foreign money flowing into the city. The rest of the world is presented the manipulated and false image of some great progressive country and unfortunately most people buy into it.

For everyone else, Islamic Sharia law is implemented, with severe punishments for what most people would consider to be very minor incidents. Workers from southern Asia and those who have no connections are dealt with in this way and can be locked away for very minor crimes. Even parking violations can result in a prison term, sometimes lasting for months.

We had all heard about the guy who was accused of making a derogatory comment about the Sheikh. After getting locked up, a quick investigation had found that there was no basis to the accusations. Unfortunately, someone forgot to inform the right person and the message got lost somewhere, the man was forgotten about for over six months. Eventually, one Police Officer listened to the man's pleas and asked his superior about the man's case and so he was finally released. The Sheikh pardoned him by gifting him a brand new, top of the range Land Cruiser SUV. So that is how things work in Dubai. Money talks and if you have it, you can pretty much do whatever you like and are immune to the Laws that the rest of us mere mortals have to be extremely wary of.

Chapter 2
Meet Daffy Duck

<u>Several hours later</u>

I sat there in complete silence for what seemed like the whole night. Boom boom boom boom. My heartbeat thumped in my ears, the only thing in the darkness that assured me I was still alive.

'Bang!' The door flew open, hitting the wall loud enough to wake the dead. A rush of cool air hit me, followed by a plethora of excited voices swarming into the room and buzzing around me like a plague of flies. A slap around my head was swiftly followed by the removal of my hood. I took a few seconds to focus properly and as my sight returned, I counted six guys facing me, all clearly very agitated. I recognised a couple of them as being part of the group of thugs who had abducted us back in the hotel, but as for the others this was the first time I was seeing them.

They started circling me, all shouting in Arabic, English or Urdu. One of them then sat on the desk in front of me and a couple pulled up chairs either side, their faces uncomfortably close to mine. A single voice broke through the noise loud and clear, as the guy directly in front of me barked,

"You tell me everything you know about the London bombing. We know you are part of the gang. You came here to hide out and you made the call. I want to know everything."

Just try and imagine for a minute somebody accusing you of such a crime. Time stops still. I just sat there looking at my accuser.

'Did he just say what I thought he did?' I said to myself.

"Tell us everything. We know what you have been involved in, it will be better for you to admit your part."

Oh my god. He really did. The room started spinning all around me and my head soon joined in, giving me a real sense that I would vomit any second. I couldn't breathe, I couldn't swallow. The men either side of me were both screaming in my face and I could see the guy at the desk was moving his mouth, but I was oblivious to everything. My eyes scanned the bare room; horrible off-white walls, no windows and no pictures. I looked down at the carpet which for some reason I had assumed was plush and expensive and saw it was cheap, nasty and covered in stains.

I'm unsure how long the interrogation went on for, as I never really lost my dazed state. Eventually they grew tired of my silence and the hood was put back over my head. The voices trailed away from me and the door slammed shut once again, leaving me to try and make some sense of what was going on. Every couple of hours they would return and the game would start again. At no point was I ever given a name, a rank, or any type of official department name for any of these guys, so I gave them my own nicknames to remember them by. Every time they had come in to question me their ID cards were turned around so I couldn't see what was written on them. I thought it a little strange, but even if they were facing the right way I wouldn't have understood what the card said, as it would be written in Arabic.

Over the next day or so, I overcame my initial shock and despite the immense fear I still felt, I realised I had to make these guys realise that they had the wrong man.

"What are you t..t ..talking about? You have it all wrong. I am not the man you are looking for." I stuttered. My throat was all dried up and my words came out in a wheezy rasp.

"What is your name?"

"Alam Ghafoor."

"No, what is your name?"

"Alam Ghafoor."

"Your middle name?"

"I don't have one."

"You lie! You have a middle name. What nationality are you?"

"British."

"No! You lie again. What nationality are you?"

"I am British. Check my passport." I looked at them puzzled as to why would they ask me twice.

"Where is your mother from?"

"Pakistan."

"And your father? Where is he from?"

"India."

"So you are Pakistani?"

"No, I am a British citizen. Please call the Embassy. I don't know what you think you know, but there has been some terrible mistake."

This conversation seemed to be repeated over and over again. I realised the interrogator was trying to wear me down, trying to make me slip up somewhere in my answers. But there would be no slip up, everything I told him was the truth.

"No, you are not British, you are a murderer. How many languages you speak?"

"English and some Urdu or Punjabi, but not very well."

"No, we know this is untrue. Why are you lying to us? We know you speak many languages."

One of the other men in the room started to speak rapidly in Arabic. He looked at me, staring hard waiting for a response, but I couldn't understand a word he said. He walked towards me, still jabbering away, the tension on his face and in his voice unable to hide the fact he was becoming very angry. He got right in my face, his spittle showering me as he grabbed me by the throat and pushed me backwards, sending me crashing to the ground.

"When was your last visit to Pakistan?"

"In 1993. I have only been there once," I answered truthfully.

"No, you have been many times. We have evidence you were at training camp in Afghanistan and also you have been to a training camp in America."

I couldn't believe what I was hearing. America? Is he joking? The only time I had been over to America was on a typical package holiday, primarily to go to Disneyland! That's hardly a terrorist training camp.

"We have the pictures."

"I want to speak to the British Embassy. I want to make a phone call, you are making a mistake, call the Embassy," I repeated once more.

The man stopped and turned to his colleague. The other man smiled and when my interrogator turned back to face me, he too had a smile on his face. He spoke assuredly.

"Why you think you are here? The British government gave us your details and told us to pick you up. We know you are the leader of the cell that just bombed London."

My mind started racing. No fucking way would the British government have us picked up. What possible reason could they have for naming me, Z, Raf or Faz? None of us have ever done anything wrong, definitely not like what our accusers are implying. And what about our families back in England? Hold on, I thought; I spoke to my sister yesterday, was it? Or the day before? I couldn't be sure how long I had been held in this room, but it wasn't more than a couple of days ago. Surely if anything was wrong she would have told me. She would have thought to mention if the authorities had raided my house.

All the time there was chatter to and fro between the two accusers, although I didn't understand a word. The tension was blatant maybe they were putting on a display for me or to each other, the machismo was way over done. Fire and hatred burned in their eyes. The conversation stopped, they both looked at me with increasing snarls the disgust was too obvious, then they stood up and left the room.

I was still on the floor, with the handcuffs digging deep into my hands, bewildered and wondering how on earth I have ended up being accused of being a terrorist bomber. A short time, maybe thirty minutes passed and the door opened, two men that I hadn't seen before came into the room. One of the men pulled me upright and then sat across from me on the other side of the desk. The other pulled up a chair and sat next to me. The one behind the desk had a round face, ironically a jolly, friendly face, with rounded John Lennon glasses. I say ironic, as it was plain to see that these guys were the next level up in interrogation and I could probably guess they had some very unfriendly methods of getting the answers they wanted to hear. He wore a full dish dash outfit complete with head covering. He stared at me for what seemed like forever, his hands steepled in front of his chest like he was going to say a prayer, but also clearly showing his position of superiority. He stuck them under his chin, kind of nodded to himself and then took a couple of slow deliberate breaths. He then spoke slowly and deliberately.

"You know why you are here?"

I shook my head from side to side.

"You are involved in the London bombings. That is why. What are you doing here in Dubai?"

"I came here on holiday and to maybe do some business."

"What business?"

"I wanted to look at the feasibility of buying property here and the possibility of eventually moving my company to Dubai."

"No, that is not the reason. When did you come here?"

"I came on the 4th July."

"Is that right? What is this on your face?"

He pointed his finger at my jaw line. When I arrived in Dubai I had heavy stubble. I looked pretty untidy. Raf said he was going to get himself a professional shave at the barbers, so with nothing better to do I went along with him and decided to have a goatee style. We had watched a Bollywood film on the plane over, the leading actor sported a goatee, so I thought for a bit of fun, I would see what one looked like on me. When we got back to our place, Z had returned from a meeting with our friend the bank manager Shad in tow, he was shocked at the change in my appearance. In his Indo-English he exclaimed, "Wow, yaar (friend) what a transformation!"

"You like it eh? I look like a film star?"

For some reason, I got a lot of attention because of my facial topiary. Afterwards, when we walked around the city, I swear people passing by on foot and in cars and buses would stare at me. Maybe they thought I was the star from the film…

"It is just a design on the beard." I said.

"NO! This is your disguise. You think you can hide, that nobody will recognise you."

I wanted to laugh at the absurdity of it all. I was a suspect purely because I'd shaved in a different way?

"No this is not a disguise. Please, I don't know what else to tell you, you are making a mistake. I am a British citizen and I want to speak to my Embassy."

Nobody seemed to understand me. British citizens have rights, everybody in the world knows that don't they? So why isn't anybody listening to me?

"Please, just let me call the Embassy and we can sort this out. I won't take it further or anything, anyone can make a mistake."

"Where do you think you are?"

With that, he sat back and looked at me unblinking. His partner had been sitting next to me quietly, still as a statue watching the conversation unfold. I had been focusing on the guy in front of me, not taking too much notice of the guy in close proximity. Leaning in closely he spoke in a low, menacing voice.

"Do you know who we are?"

I looked at him for the first time. Studied his face and the lines carefully. Thick black hair with a neat sideways parting, he looked to be around his mid-thirties. He had pale skin and strangely, almost comically exaggerated features. His mouth looked more like a ducks bill and for some reason when his mouth moved, I was reminded of daffy duck. Maybe it was the slight lisp. When he spoke he sprayed me with spittle. What is with these guys can nobody speak without spitting.

"We are the Secret Service. Not Police, not C.I.D; Secret Service", he said again proudly, as if the point needed emphasising.

"There is no law here, only what we decide. Nobody can help you, only you help yourself. We know you are part of the London gang; you came here to hide and give orders for the bomb to go off. We know everything; the British government told us to pick you up and nobody knows you are here. Nobody will speak up and say you were at Dawaat. Nobody. Do you understand that? We are going to kill you. We are going to chop you into many pieces and feed you to our dogs. There will be no trace of you at all, you disappeared that is all."

Tears rolled down my cheek as his words chilled me to the bone. All I could think of was my mother and what will she think. Would she ever accept that I just disappeared? She knows me better than that. What about my brothers and sisters? Since my father passed away, I am the head of the family. I have been in charge of everyone, as is the custom for the eldest male child. My poor son, what will become of him? What will he make of this, his daddy went away to make things better, to make some money and he just disappeared never to be heard from again. Kids being kids, is he going to grow up hating himself because of something he imagined he did that pushed me away? Or worse, maybe the story will come out and he will believe that I was some insane terrorist who died because of some terrible acts I was supposed to have performed. How will my boy live with that?

My heart was pounding as these thoughts cascaded through my mind. What about that bastard fortune teller I'd been to see when we'd had a trip to the seaside; he told me I would live to 80. Maybe he read the wrong fucking palm.

"You are evil!" I was slapped hard across the face.

"You are a very bad man. Go ahead and cry. Cry for the innocent people you have murdered."

This time a punch followed the tirade.

"You kill people and now is your turn to suffer. Cry for yourself, for you can help yourself. Tell us the truth and maybe you won't have to die. But you will never leave here."

"My mother had a heart attack last year. I don't want my disappearance to give her another one. Please let me call her. Let me make one phone call."

"No. First you must tell us the truth and I mean everything….I am your brother," he said with his voice softening, he patted his chest "I want to help you… I will help, but you are going to stay here for ten, maybe twenty years. We will give you pain, you will beg us to kill you, you will wish for your own end. If you are lucky, then maybe you will have a heart attack and that will stop your pain."

My chest tightened by the second. I suffer from hay fever and sometimes it's bad enough that I need an inhaler. The stress was getting to me now and I needed it desperately.

"Please, I have some medication that I need. It is just an inhaler; can you get it for me?"

"Later …later ….we will leave you to think, think about what we said. We will come back later."

With that, the two men stood up and left the room, leaving me to think over what they had just said. The bastards. How can they threaten me like this? Surely the British Government would not have any reason to raid my house, even if they did, they wouldn't find anything to link me to any terrorists. I have never done anything wrong in my life. The nearest I've gotten to any kind of subversive behaviour was attending a Socialist Worker party meeting when I was studying sociology at college.

Mr Sudan and The Fat Man

Sitting in that room, I could feel nothing except total and utter despair. Time meant nothing to me. There were no clocks or windows to give me any idea of how long I had been there. Was it just hours? Or was it days? Eventually the door opened once more and in came two fairly elderly guys. The first one who entered was huge; maybe 6 '4 and quite heavily built. He looked to me like he was maybe Sudanese, somewhere between African and Arabic. His head was big and square and coupled with his large broad nose, he reminded me of the statues from Easter Island. The man who followed him inside the room was a big guy too. He was over six feet tall and carried a lot of weight around his middle. His belly leading him by a good eight inches or so He was pale skinned, clean shaven and had a couple of spare chins. For some reason they didn't seem as intimidating as the previous two evil bastards I'd encountered, although I wasn't planning on getting my hopes up just yet. They each took a seat, spoke quietly to each other in Arabic and then shuffled through a pile of papers that they each had in their hands. Finally, they looked at me.

"You look frightened. There is no need. What is problem?" Mr Sudan said softly.

"Your guys told me I am to be killed by the morning, for this crime you accuse me of."

"Which guys?"

"The ones who were here earlier. The ones who slapped me around and said I have done terrible things. But it is not true, I swear."

"No, no. Don't worry. We will not kill you," he said with a half-hearted laugh. His words inspired little confidence in me.

"Let me get you a drink," the Fat man said, rising from his chair.

He went out for a minute or two while Sudan stared at me, trying to read my face, like the answer or solution to this mess was hidden there, waiting to be uncovered, the belly came in along with Fat man he waddled over and handed me a small cup of water. Sitting down, he shuffled his papers again and spoke.

"So, Alam. What exactly are you doing here? When did you come to Dubai?"

"I came here on the 4th July for business and a short holiday. I have done nothing wrong. I am a British citizen and I want to speak to my Embassy"

"Yes, yes. Later Alam. Now tell me… you like it here in Dubai?"

"Yes I do. Or should I say did. I think it is a very nice place, but now you are accusing me of this crime and I don't like it so much."

"Do you drink alcohol?"

"No, I do not."

"Are you sure Alam? Are you lying?"

"I tried it a couple of times in England when I was younger, but not for years and not in Dubai. I have no reason to lie about that."

"We know you drink a Johnnie Walker bottle every time you go Seashells Hotel."

"You are mistaken. If you check with the staff they will tell you I only drink water. No Coke, no red bull and definitely no Johnnie Walker. Every time I have been they put a bottle of water out for me."

Fat man shook his head. A murmur of a smile on his face

"One of my men has seen you. It is stupid to lie about this Alam. If you lie to me now, how can I believe anything else you say to me?"

I thought back to every night out in Dubai. But why was I bothering? I knew for certain I had never had a drink in Seashells, or anywhere else in Dubai for that matter. Then the last thing Fat man had said to me suddenly registered in my brain, 'one of my men has seen you....'

I had a kind of flashback and remembered that one of the shorter bastards who had pulled us out of Dawaat had looked vaguely familiar. I was sure I knew that face from somewhere. I was sure it was somehow connected to a previous time at the club. And then it came to me. He was in a dish dash, he was with a few other guys, throwing cards and generally having a good time. At the end of the night there was an argument between him and the management because of the bill, he had refused to pay up. After creating a scene his little gang walked out and nobody tried or dared to stop them. I asked somebody who he was and they brushed it off as another local idiot with too much money and too many connections.

"Did you pay money to the band so you could sleep with the girls?" Mr Sudan barked at me, snapping me out of trance.

I wanted to say what I really thought but decided it best that I keep my thoughts to myself. You what? Did I pay money? You have got to be fucking joking; I wouldn't pay for those slappers! What do you think I am, fucking desperate?

"No. I have never given any money to any band."

"What do you know about the London bombing?"

"I was in my hotel room at the Hilton Deira Creek, room 101 when I heard about it. My friend Raf was staying with me, as we had travelled here together. Our friend Z, who had been living here, had come to pick us up, we were going out for lunch. While were watching the television, Z had a phone call. He told us that bombs had gone off in London, so we switched over to Sky TV News and saw the live pictures."

"What did you think?"

"First of all they were saying they thought it was power failure, but then it was confirmed it was bombs."

"So what did you think?" Sudan repeated.

"What did I think? I thought it was bloody awful. I have friends and family in London, all I could think was I hope they are all safe," I replied agitatedly.

"How did you feel?" Sudan said, ignoring my little outburst.

"I just told you how I felt. I was worried for my family and friends."

"So what did you do next?"

"We watched the news for a little longer, I phoned my sister to make sure everyone was safe and to ask what was happening and to...."

"Why you calling sister?" Fat man interrupted.

"When bombs go off anywhere, the Muslims are the first to be accused by people, even before any kind of confirmation of what has happened. People start abusing anybody they think is a Muslim."

Sudan scanned his paperwork for a few seconds, read something to himself under his breath, gave a slight shake of his head and then looked back at me.

"You asked your sister if everything is alright. What exactly did you mean by that?"

"I always ask her that every time we speak. She runs her own store so I ask about that and everything in general."

"No, you asked there is no trouble?"

"Yes, I did ask her that. I meant has there been any problems because the family are Muslim and have there been any more bombs that have gone off in different towns, that may not have yet made the international news."

"Why? Did you plan other towns to be bombed?"

"I didn't plan anything. I am not a bomber."

"When did you go to training camp in Afghanistan?"

"I have never been to Afghanistan and I have never attended any training camp."

"You have been to Pakistan yes, many times?"

"No, only once. Look, we are going round in circles. I can't tell you about things that I have no knowledge of. I want to speak to the Embassy please; this is all a big mistake."

"Yes, you can speak later...they know you are here."

For several more hours, the questioning continued. Back and forth, back and forth. Different interrogators came and went, asking the same questions, making the same accusations and me giving the same answers.

****

Z

I sat in the back of the car wondering what the hell was going on. I heard the engine switch off and the car door opening. The muffled grunts and rocking of the car made it apparent that Alam was being taken away. I sat there for a few moments wondering when it would be my turn. I called out to Alam, but got no reply. I just sat there going over and over what was happening. What possible reason there could be that got us in this predicament. I couldn't hear anyone in the car, or even just outside. I remember wondering if they had forgotten about me. Should I try and get the blindfold off? Try and get a peep at where I was?

Before I got a chance to test my bravery, the car door opened and I was dragged out of my seat and led away. My knees buckled under me and so whoever was leading me had to manhandle me across the ground and up a couple of steps into an air-conditioned building. I heard voices muttering as I was led through a door and down a stone corridor. Footsteps echoed off the walls as we walked. I could tell we were in a very narrow passageway. I could also tell that the men carrying me wore heavy Army boots. When one sense is taken from you, people always say that your others seem to be enhanced somehow, so I had an idea in my mind of the kind of facility I was in, despite my lack of sight. We stopped suddenly, there was a jangle of keys and then a heavy iron door creaked open. The men dragged me to a chair and pushed me down into it. Without a word, they left the room, locked the door and left me sitting there with my cuffs and blindfold still on. I waited a few minutes and then I tried to get my blindfold off, but to no avail. I shouted out,

"Alam! Raf! Are you there? Do you hear me?" But there was no answer. God only knows how long I sat there, but finally I heard keys turning in the lock. The door creaked open and someone entered the room. The blindfold was pulled off me and as my eyes adjusted to the light, two mean looking men came slowly into focus.

"Who are you? Why am I here?" I asked.

They didn't identify themselves and they didn't answer my questions. They simply told me that my friends had been arrested and I had better tell them everything I know. It was not made clear exactly what it was that they wanted me to explain, but before I could press them any further they just got up and left. Another twenty minutes or so went by and two other men came into the room. They asked me the same questions. What do you know? Tell us everything. But once again, they never clarified exactly what it was that I should be telling them about. They stated that I was not being held in a Police station, I was in fact in the hands of the National Security Secret Service of Dubai. They made it very clear that nobody knew where we were and that they had the power to hold me for one day, a week, a year or twenty years. Depending on my assistance and answers, maybe I would be released at some point. I asked if I could make a phone call to the Consulate and to my wife to notify them of my well-being, but they ignored me. And then they got up and left.

Another hour or so passed by, maybe longer. Two different men came in, bringing a load of paperwork with them. I asked if somebody can tell me what is going on here? Only to be told,

"Shut up and listen very carefully. You need to explain why you are here in Dubai, what you have been doing and what you did before you arrived. We don't have to explain anything to you."

And so began a long list of questions. They asked for my name, my address and what was my business. How long had I been living here. How did I obtain residency. They asked me over and over again and each time, all I could say were the same answers. Then they started asking more in depth questions regarding my business affairs, who my customers were, who my suppliers were, who did I bank with here in Dubai and what about the UK. I was questioned like this for a couple of hours, then they suddenly stopped. One guy shuffled his papers, nodded to the other, then stood up to leave. He leaned in close to me and whispered.

"One last thing you should know. Your phone calls have been recorded for over six months. So don't think about lying to us."

The other guy just looked at me, slowly nodding his head, as if to say, 'listen to what the man says.' Then he too stood up and together they left.

Ten or so minutes later, the guy who had kidnapped me from Seashells came in. Holding up a piece of paper, he told me,

"This is for you to sign, giving permission for the Dubai Police to search your apartment. If you have nothing to hide, then sign it. If you don't we will search anyway and with less respect for your stuff, you understand me?"

He placed the paper on the desk and took a pen from his pocket.

"Go on, sign."

I signed the paper without looking at it and sat back down in my chair. Somebody else came into the room, blindfolded me once more and led me out of my cell. Back in the corridor again, I tried my best to hear Alam, Raf or Faz, but all I heard was the scraping of my captors boots on the stone floor. Another door opened and suddenly I took a breath of the hot evening air deep into my lungs

"Come. Come," said an agitated voice, as I was frogmarched along. I was pushed into the back of a car, squashed in the middle with a guard on either side of me. I was driven some distance before the blindfold was removed. Familiar roads soon came into view and I realised where we were going. Upon reaching my apartment, another vehicle was already waiting outside. All seven Police, or Detectives, or whatever they were, accompanied me into my apartment. Once inside they carried out what can only be described as a very detailed search. If you have ever seen films and thought you could find somewhere to hide things, somewhere that no-one would think of looking, then I'm sorry to burst your bubble. These guys search everywhere. Every food packet was opened, every tin can, every drawer, cupboard and floorboard. Holes were drilled in walls and camera's inserted. It was beyond scary. They searched every room, taking away any business files, mobile phones, or computer equipment. Clothing was piled up and seams were checked, small incisions made. Then they came out of Alam's room with his suitcase. They took the clothing out and dumped it on the floor and as I watched what happened next, my mouth fell open, my heart rate raised several notches and I literally had to lean against the wall to steady myself. The Officer took out a knife and sliced the lining. He looked up and smiled at me. He then ripped the rest of the lining off and held the case up, to show me and the rest of his men the line of long blue cartons covered in cellophane, carefully arranged around the inside of the suitcase.

The officer took them out one by one and started carefully laying them out on the table. At this point I was taken out of the room. All I could think was that it looked like bundles of Semtex or some other explosive.

We were at the apartment for another couple of hours before they had everything they wanted. I was led outside, sat back in the car with my guards and blindfolded once more. Eventually the car started up and off we went again. The men in the car with me chattered away for most of the drive, obviously very happy with their discovery. But I didn't really take much in, too distraught at what probably lay ahead for us all. The car pulled up some time later and like déjà vu I was dragged into the building with the stone floors, frogmarched down a corridor and placed back in a cell.

****

Raf

Eventually I was dragged from the car and taken into a building. I was thrown into a cell, my handcuffs were removed and blindfold taken off. I think I was in there until the early morning, as I am sure I heard birds singing to welcome the new day. Someone came in and without saying a word, I was cuffed and blindfolded and taken to another room. I was pushed into a chair and told to sit still, be quiet and wait for someone to come for me. So I just sat there in silence, with my hands cuffed and blindfold on wondering what the hell this was all about.

The door flew open, making me jump almost out of my skin. I heard four voices, all shouting at once, the cacophony of noise too much for me to take any words in. Someone grabbed me roughly and pulled off my blindfold. Four guys were standing over me, looking very menacing. All at once they started shouting and screaming at me, demanding information about the bombing; who, where and when etc. The aggressive manner and abusive language spilt over into rage. I was punched and kicked around the room, my shirt was ripped off my back and I was told in no uncertain terms that I was about to die. If I wanted to live I had better give them the information they said they knew I possessed. I was in the room for many hours, maybe even a full day or two constantly threatened with beatings and death. After a while I just felt numb, as if I was in some kind of nightmare from which I couldn't wake up.

Chapter 3
Killing Mickey

Alam

I was in the cell, a small oblong white-washed room, barely six feet by nine, with a single wafer-thin mattress perched on a concrete platform that laughably passed for a bed. There was nothing else in the room, but at least there was a tiny slit high up on the wall, about the size of a letterbox through which sunlight streamed. It may not seem like much, but just being aware of whether it was night or day gave me small comfort. I lay back on the mattress, trying not to focus on the stains or the smell and was surprised to see that, over the door was a small portable TV fixed to the wall and inside a sturdy cage. How had I missed that? It wasn't tuned in properly so there was more of a buzz than any intelligible noise coming from it. The picture was blurry and kept on distorting further, like it was doing a little dance as it swung first to the left and then to the right. Still, it was better than laying in silence. I could just about make out in the bottom corner of the screen the time it was 8.30. I sat up, put my head in my hands and tried to imagine the news back home...

'Today in Dubai three British nationals were arrested

in connection with the London bombings. Security services swooped late on Wednesday evening and took the men away for questioning. A spokesperson gave an official statement confirming the arrests and said that the National Security Service is dealing with the men accordingly. One of the men arrested is Alam Ghafoor from Huddersfield, Yorkshire. His family run a small shop in the town, they have refused to comment over the allegations. In what Police believe to be a related incident, the family business was fire-bombed late last night.'

Horrible thoughts, but they kept turning over in my mind. All different scenarios of how my situation may be perceived, the interviews with neighbours saying 'he seemed such a nice man...kept himself to himself....always polite...who would have thought?'

I shuddered...no, it's not possible; once the British Government know I am here, they will realise I am not a terrorist.

I heard a noise outside in the corridor and turned my head to look at the door. It wasn't heavy Army boots like I would have expected, it was more like the shuffle of sandals along the stone floor. The noise stopped outside my door, a key was put into the lock and with a click click and a clunk, the heavy door wheezed open.

"Come." The man said.

As I stepped out of the cell, he placed a blindfold on me again and then I was dragged along the corridor.

'Here we go again,' I thought to myself, 'I wonder where they're going to take me now?'

I fully expected to be taken to the same interrogation room as before, but I heard another metal door scrape open and realised I was walking down a new corridor. The door slammed shut behind me, my escort muttered something to another man, who answered with a deep gravelly voice.

"Come, walk." He said once more.

It wasn't like I was struggling or anything, so his prompting was unnecessary. It's just that when you can't see a thing and the person holding your arm is not your friend, you are automatically wary of your footing. So you walk hesitantly, feeling out every step as you go, as if you are walking through a minefield I guess. We turned several corners and walked more corridors. Damn, how big is this place?

Finally, we stopped once more, my guide chatted with another man. I knew I should have learned Arabic. I made a pledge to myself right there and then that if I ever got out of this place I would make an effort to learn such an important and widespread language. I heard another door open and I was pushed forward and through the threshold. I almost fell over, as my feet felt all spongy on the new surface. I realised it was just a thick carpet that cushioned my steps. Strange thoughts enter your mind at the strangest of times and I remember thinking right then that I had been in my trainers since we left the apartment on the Wednesday evening and my feet must be reeking by now.

The inevitable happened and I was pushed into a chair, my blindfold was removed. I sat there staring at the walls awaiting my fate. The walls were blank; no pictures, no clocks, just an ugly desk in front of me just like my previous interrogation room. In fact, I was sure it was identical. Maybe they bought a job lot? I smiled to myself at the inane suggestion. One noticeable difference to the previous room, other than the plush carpet, was the temperature. My first interrogation room had felt positively air-conditioned compared to this one, which was like an oven.

I heard voices going back and forth outside the room. They would sound as if they were coming towards my door and then they would taper off into the distance. There appeared to be a constant shuffle of sandals coming and going in the corridor which made me think that this was a busy day. I quickly became used to the noise outside, almost to the point of not looking at the door every time sandals passed by. Eventually I heard the shuffling stop dead outside the room and after a jangle of heavy keys and a click, click, clunk, the door flew open.

Moonface and Daffy Duck came in. Moonface went straight round to the other side of the desk, sat down and looked through some notes. Daffy pulled a chair out from behind the desk and sat next to me. He stared at my face for a minute or so before he spoke.

"So, Alam. You have had time to think about everything. Tell me what you know? How did you know about the bombing? How did you know how many bombs were used?"

I began repeating verbatim exactly what I told him a few hours earlier.

"Yes, yes you told me all this before, Alam. I want to know more."

"I don't know any more about it. How can I tell you what I do not know?"

"Tell me Alam, do you pray?"

"Yes I pray."

"How many times a day?"

"I pray as much as I can," I answered truthfully.

"And you go to Friday prayers?"

"Yes I go. Sometimes I miss them, but I try not to."

"So is this how Muslims live in England?"

"Life is hectic. Unfortunately it happens sometimes that it is not possible to make every prayer time."

"You know you should pray five times a day, don't you Alam?"

"Yes, of course."

"Then why don't you?"

"I don't live in a Muslim country. Sometimes I have business to do and I can't arrange everything around my prayer times. Non-Muslims don't understand such things."

"This is your reasoning?"

"If I told you I prayed five times a day, every day, does that make me a terrorist? Now, because I don't, I am still a terrorist? What has this to do with anything!"

"You speak Arabic?"

"No."

"Why you no speak Arabic? You read Quran?"

"Yes, I read it a lot when I was younger, but my Arabic needs more practise."

"So you speak Arabic?"

"No I don't speak it. We are taught to read Arabic from the Quran but we don't learn how to speak it."

"What do you mean?"

"A teacher will tell us how the words are recited, to get the correct pronunciation. So we learn to read it and the meaning is explained to us in Punjabi or Urdu."

"That is strange." Daffy shook his head and scrunched his face in disgust. His upper lip unable to hide the yellowing teeth.

Yes it was strange, but that was the way it was done and probably still is in many parts of the world. The only problem with this practise is that it leads to teachers telling their students the meanings and interpretations as they see them. That is not a bad thing by default, but you always have the risk that a hard-line fundamentalist teacher can manipulate their pupils, as seen in some religious schools in Pakistan, Afghanistan and Indonesia over the last few years.

"Are you married?"

"No. I was engaged once and I have a son."

I could see the look of indignation when I told him of my son and the fact that I hadn't been married. But, I had no reason to lie. Thinking back I should have done so to save myself further aggravation. I took an instant dislike to this self-righteous bastard from the first time I met him and now that was growing into pure hatred. Just who the fuck did he think he was, to judge me or anybody else?

"Please, let me call the British Embassy? I have nothing more to tell you."

Daffy finally spoke, breaking the long silent pause but the look of disgust was still on his face.

"The British know you are here; they told us to pick you up. They gave us the information about you, now you have to give us information. So, tell me what you know."

"Oh change the record," I snapped, "I said I don't know anything!"

"Now then, Alam, that's...."

Moonface interrupted Daffy with a raise of his hand. They swapped chairs and Moonface pulled his new chair real close to mine. He spoke in a gentle, matter-of-fact way. His tone never wavered.

"It is not a problem. Later today we have special people coming to see you. They will make you talk. Believe me; their speciality is in making people talk. I am trying to help you but, I don't think you want my help. I am a very kind man."

"Yes, I can see you are very kind. I thank you for being so kind," I said in my most sarcastic voice, although it was clearly lost on Moonface.

"You want my help? Then talk, talk now."

"Look, I don't know anything about any bombs. I told you plenty of times; I am here on holiday and to register a business. That's the truth and it's not going to change."

Daffy suddenly looked up at me and glared. His nose twitched and without taking his eyes off me, he screwed up his face like he had discovered something utterly revolting.

"What is the smell?" He shouted

He moved towards me and sniffed the air. He reminded me of a bloodhound with his exaggerated sniffing

"Yes, it is you. You smell. You smell dirty. You dirty Pakistani. Move away from me. Get up out of the chair."

I stood up and he beckoned me to move away, so slowly I walked backwards.

"Go on, go back there. Stand by the wall."

I did as I was told. I smelled myself and yes I really did stink.

"You haven't let me wash, it is hot in here," I protested. "I've been sweating in these same clothes for God only knows how long."

"Don't talk …don't talk to me …you animal."

He looked at Moonface. They held eye contact for a minute or so, then both burst out laughing, jabbering away in Arabic. Daffy looked at me and his laughter stopped. He rushed over to me and slapped me hard across the face.

"Look at the floor, you animal," he said, with an abhorrent look on his face.

He spat at me, spraying my face with his spittle and then walked out of the room. Moonface sat completely emotionless, just glaring at me.

"You are going to be here for a long time. A very long time, Mr Alam. Maybe twenty years, if you survive that long. But you will not get lonely; every-day I will come to see you. I will be like family to you, but in the evening I will go home to my house with my family and forget about you. You will never see your family again and they will think you are dead. I will be the only person you will know in the world, the only person you will ever see. Every day you will beg to die but I won't let you die. But believe me, you will be punished. If you don't want this to happen, then tell us everything. Tell us how this happened and who are the people involved. I will go now, so you have time to think. Think about what you have done, so that when I come back you tell me."

I stood there, still up against the wall, like a naughty schoolboy. I was sweating profusely, like the room temperature had risen even higher than before, which I guess it had with the extra body heat. Moonfaces' cold words went round and round in my head.

You will be here for twenty years.

You will never see your family again.

We can kill you and nobody will ever know.

I stood there swaying uneasily, but, not bothering to sit back down. More voices outside, more shuffling of sandals. My door opened again and in walked Mr Sudan and another man, who looked like a miniature version of the fat man from yesterday.

"'Salaam, how are you?"

"Ok."

"You are Ok? Here, you want a drink?"

I was given a small cup of water. Always small cups for god's sake don't you guys have regular size cups. I sipped slowly from the tiny cup and watched as my captors set up for the next round of questioning. These guys must learn their techniques from some special interrogator's school or something. By now, I knew exactly how this was going to play out, as if I had a script in front of me. Ok then, here goes...and there we have it. Mr Sudan sits behind the desk, flicks through and then shuffles a pile of papers. Check one. Mini fat man will pull a chair up close to mine, close enough so I can smell his body odour and stare at me menacingly, while Sudan asks me the same questions for the umpteenth time.

Mr mini fat man - maybe a cousin or a brother of yesterday's inquisitor – looked just like the big version in every way, except for his stature and lack of designer stubble. This wasn't right, I thought. He was deviating from the script! He stood directly in front of me holding his phone horizontally in front of his chest. The ear piece was plugged in and he held it tightly as if somebody was going to snatch it off him. I heard muffled voices from the earpiece. Mini fat man nodded several times, looking at me, then looking away. Finally he said something in Arabic, took the wire from his ear and spoke to me.

"How much money you have?"

"I don't really have anything more than the money I have here in Dubai."

I didn't want to say too much because these guys are well known for taking backhanders and the more they think they can get from you, the more they will ask for.

"Really? You are a business man are you not? You must have plenty of money."

"No, I do not. I have many business loans and a large

mortgage that is very expensive. Any money I or my family make, we put together to help each other."

Sudan butted in, "Yes we do same here…you have many properties?"

At this point I wasn't sure if I should be totally honest with them or not, so I decided to play it safe for now. I didn't know where this conversation was going, so best to downplay things for the moment.

"No, I have the house that I live in and I was hoping to buy one in America, if I could raise the funds."

"You like America? Do you go?"

"Yes I had a good time, I went to Disneyland"

"Where?"

"You know... Mickey Mouse?"

"No. What is this?"

"It is an amusement park, it is world famous."

"Oh Ok. So, how you afford to buy a house?"

"I have a mortgage. I like the house, so I pay a deposit, the bank lend me the rest of the money and then I pay them back every month for thirty years and the house is mine."

Absolutely crazy. I had to explain to the guys how a mortgage worked.

"How will you buy second house?"

"If the price has gone up, like many prices have already gone up, then you can re-mortgage the house and the spare money you can borrow back and use elsewhere."

"Ahh. But you will have to pay more money back?"

"Yes, you only borrow if you can make the new bigger payment."

I couldn't believe this. I was giving these idiots a lecture in how to refinance your house and create a portfolio of properties. They carried on asking more questions regarding financing of houses and avidly took notes. I explained how a group of us had clubbed together and pooled our money by refinancing in this way. We had used the money to purchase a few properties in Dubai. I said properties, but the truth was that the properties were still a good two to three years off from being built and as things stood, we had so far just paid for sand.

The two men went quiet for a couple of minutes. Both scribbled in their notepads, a couple of times they said something to each other, then scribbled some more. I thought to myself that maybe they wanted to invest some money in our company and were just working out how much spare capital they could raise?

Fatty soon burst my bubble.

"You live in England. Is it good? You like?"

"Yes it is very nice."

"You not marry? Why? You are gay?"

"No, I am not gay."

"Why no marry?"

"I have girlfriend."

"You have girlfriend? Oh of course, you say you have a son, yes?"

"Yes, I do."

"So you have a son, but you are not married?"

"Yes."

"Why you not married?"

"It's complicated."

"What is complicated? Life is not complicated, it is simple," he nodded his head in agreement with himself. Yeah thanks for the philosophy on life, I thought.

The phone lit up in Fatty's hand and he reattached the earpiece. He softened his tone and whispered into it smiling. He got up and left the room. Sudan sat there, shuffling his papers. We sat in silence for several minutes and I wondered if he would wait for his colleague to return before continuing with the questioning. Maybe protocol or something. I was taken by surprise when he suddenly said,

"Alam I want to help you, tell me why you came here to Dubai?"

"I told you, I am here on holiday and I wanted to set up a business. Please let me speak to the Embassy"

"Yes later. Are you Ok? Do you like Dubai?"

"No I am not Ok; you have made a wrong arrest. I don't like it here. You have the wrong man and I just want to go home."

"Don't worry you will have your business, you will get out in one day."

He left. I wasn't sure if I heard that correctly. Was it one day as in the following day? Or one day, as in one day eventually? My spirits lifted anyway. I'm sure he said in one day and I thought thank god the Embassy must have got involved and told them it was all a mistake. I was going to be out of here in a day or so. The lock double–clicked; a sound that will forever be imprinted on my mind.

A skinny guy came in and blindfolded me, cuffed me and led me away. I stumbled a little, but was now getting used to being led this way. One gate slammed and then the other. I was soon back in the warm corridor going towards my original cell. We stopped around the place that I had guessed we would; the blindfold was taken off, the cuffs removed, then he pushed me into the cell, slamming the door shut. I hadn't thought about it, but up until this point I had only been given a tiny drink of water and a small carton of orange juice. It's funny how you lose your appetite when faced with twenty years imprisonment or death. Not much of a choice.

Sitting staring at the white wall with the TV buzzing away in the background. To my right a small plastic box had been left in the cell but there was nothing in it, so I positioned it under the TV and was just able to reach up and tune it the best I could. I sat down and was happy to see it had improved the picture a little. Small victories taste just as sweet. I sat down on the edge of the bed and happened to look up at the air vent above the TV. It was filthy dirty, but I could definitely make out a shape sitting immediately behind. I supposed it must be a camera or something, which was no real surprise. I ignored it and started to watch the box. I flicked through the limited amount of channels until I happened to stop on a program called Fat Club or something like that. The guy was being congratulated on having lost thirty pounds of fat and as a reward he was allowed to have something very precious; his kids were allowed to visit him.

Tears formed in my eyes and soon I was blubbing like a baby. I cried for my little boy; oh how I missed him. Maybe this was my punishment for having clipped him round the ear a couple of weeks earlier. We had been reading together and he wasn't paying attention, but thinking back, what do you expect from a seven year old? I flicked his ear, his little face scrunched and he started crying, "Mummy never hits me. Why are you hitting me and shouting at me Daddy? I wasn't born to be treated like this."

I felt like such a horrible bastard. How I wish I could have taken that moment back. I used to speak to him every day, no matter where I was and every weekend he would come and stay with me. With tears still streaming down my face, I said a little prayer and sent my love to him.

I had been dating Vicky for a couple of years. She also had a little boy from a previous relationship. She was a really good and decent girl, a great friend and confidant. Her only downfall was whenever the shit hit the fan; she would turn to her other best friend el vino. That had been the main reason for our recent problems. The more we argued the more she drank. And the more I pulled her up on her drinking, the unhappier she got and you can imagine this led to more drinking. I pictured her sitting there quietly seething, thinking that if he can't be bothered to ring, maybe it's all over between us. Then I thought of Ann, who was my son's mother. She would think that I don't want to see my son. I had a horrible idea of her telling my boy that Daddy was too busy to call or see him, so forget about him, he's not worth crying over. I had this terrible vision that maybe I would be here for twenty years and eventually I would get out and make my way to England to find everybody had forgotten me.

I would go to my sister's shop and find everybody had moved away. My mother would had passed away after having another heart attack, brought about by the mysterious disappearance of her son. And eventually, if I could find my son, he would not recognise me or believe I was his father. And even with the small chance that he would; who's to say he would want anything to do with me?

How had things come to this? It was only a few days ago that I had been thinking how grateful I was for the opportunity to travel and stay in fine hotels and do the work that I loved to do. Also how I had got back on my feet after some poor business ventures.. I set up a business a year ago, the aim being to promote talented local teenagers to all the mainstream TV channels and get these kids into work on both sides of the camera, as presenters and technical help. Most of them had some amateur experience and had been involved in some way on a local level, either with hospital radio, pirate stations or independent film-making. Well I had sunk some of my own money into the business to get it up and running and my business partner kept promising to match it when this person paid, or that cheque cleared. But somehow no money ever materialised. My partner managed to spend all our cash on 'expenses' and then the phone number I had for him went mysteriously offline. Last thing I heard about this 'friend' was that he was promoting two-bit bands around the north of England, ripping off others as he went, bragging about being the talent spotter for the BBC. I had laughed when I thought about it; here I was travelling the world doing business on a much bigger scale..

I realised that tears still streamed down my face. I hadn't cried like this since my father passed away. Eventually I composed myself and lay back on the bed. Damn it was hot in there. I put my hand up to the tiny ventilation grill and, surprise surprise, the air con was not working. There was an intercom on the wall, so I pressed it and waited.

I put my ear to the com and was surprised to hear it crackle, followed by a mumbling voice. I couldn't make out what was said, so I pressed the button again and asked for water. The intercom went off and a few minutes later I heard flip flop, flip flop, swoosh. Click click clunk. The heavy cell door opened.

"Come."

I stepped out the door, expecting to be blindfolded and cuffed, but the man pushed me along the corridor a little way to a flask in the middle of the floor. Sunlight from a tiny window washed over the flask, giving it an ethereal glow as I approached it. My escort stuck his head inside another door and someone inside must have passed him an empty water bottle. I don't know how old it was or what it had been used for before, but I gratefully took it from him and filled it from the flask. I was then led back to the cell and forcefully pushed back inside. I sat down and took a swig of water. Aaaargh! Disgusting! The water was almost boiling and had a stale, unpleasant taste to it. But I had no choice; I needed water, so I had to drink it. I put my drink down and stared around my cell. I looked at the letterbox sized window high up on the wall and jumped up and down on the mattress a couple of times until I managed to cling on to the grill with my fingertips. With some difficulty, I pulled myself up until I could just peer outside. I could see a courtyard, but it was surrounded on all four sides by high walls. My fingers were killing me with the strain of my whole body weight. I lost my grip and fell back onto the mattress. I turned my attention to the vent for the air-con and noticed the lens again. So grabbing the plastic box again and carefully balancing on it, I tried to get a closer look. I was certain it was a CCTV camera, but I couldn't see a red light or anything. Do they all have a light? And if so, maybe it wasn't recording right now. Well that was it, the whole cell had been explored and there was nothing else to do, but to go back to my negative thoughts.

To try and remain positive in such a situation was harder than I would ever have imagined. I decided I had to at least try and help myself, so I repeated the famous Emile Cou saying 'day by day, every day; life is getting better and better.' I remembered reading about Charlie Bronson, the strongest and most-feared prisoner in the UK. I had read about how he did hundreds of press ups and sit-ups every day and was feared by screws and lags alike. If I was to be in here for a long time, then I would strive for excellence and become the strongest and most feared in my new world. I did thirty or so squats and knocked out twenty press-ups. Not a bad start, I thought. My overall mood brightened and I started to feel a little better. Exercise always lifts the spirits

I must have been in the cell for a couple of hours. The TV had distorted again, so much so that I couldn't see the time. I couldn't really sleep. I stank so badly I even made myself retch a few times. The air-con had not been turned back on and it was so hot in there I felt like I was slowly being cooked. Flip flops approached. Two clicks and a clunk.

"Get up."

I got up and the man beckoned me to the door. He swung me round and put a blindfold on me.

"Come."

Off we went, back to the interrogation room.

The same questions were fired at me; name, address, citizenship origin etc. etc. I was tiring of answering them, but figured maybe they still thought they could catch me out. Different teams would come in, with some guys I had not seen before, but all asking the exact same questions.

Chapter 4
Waxing da booty

It had been a while since my last outing. I jumped when the door swung open and a single guy came in, one that I had not seen before. He was probably in his late twenties, was very well built and well groomed with the obligatory designer stubble on a surprisingly friendly looking face. It was obvious he worked out, as his dish dash strained to hold his muscles, looking rather like a condom stuffed with walnuts. He sat in the chair and swivelled side to side. Eventually he looked up at me, pulled a few faces deciding which one would get the better response and asked quite politely if I wanted a drink of water. I nodded.

Easing himself out of the chair slowly, he walked off like John Wayne. Locked the door behind himself, but returned just as quickly. Thrusting into my eager hand a couple of sealed cups of water, like the ones you get on the plane with your meal. I gulped them down one after the other.

"I know they have been giving you a hard time," he said softly.

His English wasn't bad; there were the usual Arabic undertones, making him sound like a mix of Middle Eastern meets MTV.

"I am not here to question you Alam. I wanted to get you a break. I work as a clerk here and I have to do all the typing and filing. I have been reading through your file."

I had heard enough bullshit over the last couple of days, so I wasn't going to get all excited at what was probably just another game. Keeping a blank face no emotion I just looked at him, saying nothing. A long silence followed.

"I don't think you are a bad man. I don't believe you are involved in terrorist activities, but I can't say anything to my superiors. I would like you to help yourself and get out of here. It is not a good place for you."

Ok, I thought. Maybe they have sent him in to try the old good cop, bad cop routine. They really must think I am stupid. I don't have anything to hide and surely they know that by now, so what is this bollocks they're playing at. I thought Ok, I will play along.

"Have you ever been to England?" I asked him.

"No. I don't really have a desire to go there, I usually go to Thailand for my holidays," he smiled.

"Thailand?"

"Yes, it is good. The chicks are hot and totally crazy!"

"Really?"

"Yes, but I haven't been now for two years now, not since I got married. I used to go two or three times a year with my friends."

"You are married, that's good." I nodded.

"You are not married?" he asked. He already said that he has seen all my notes, so he should know the answer to that. Still, I'll play along.

"No, but I have a girlfriend."

"In England there is no problem?"

"No problem."

"Tell me… English girls ….they are hot?"

"Yes some of them are very hot."

"They have good bodies, heh?" He put his hands in front of his chest.

"They have big?"

"Yes, some of them have big ones."

"I see on television, but many they look fat. Fat bodies and legs I don't like," he said, shaking his head from side to side.

"You know I like to wax the booty," he said out of the blue.

I wanted to laugh out loud; the conversation was beyond surreal, especially him using a term like that. All thanks to MTV and its sexy hip hop videos.

"Waxing the booty is good," I told him

"They like fucking?"

"Yes I guess they do."

"Hummm."

"You still go out with your friends now you are married?"

"Yes of course. Sometimes we go for a meal, then smoke sheesha at the beach. Sometimes we go to parties with the air hostesses; they are seriously hot and they like to fuck and go crazy. I wax the booty man, the girls are from all over the world we meet at the Carlton Hotel."

I couldn't help laughing. In any other situation, I would think he was a pretty cool guy. He told me all about his wife, his mother and father. He brought me more water and even a carton of mango juice. The sweet taste made me feel light headed, it was the most beautiful drink I think I had ever tasted. I don't know how long he was there with me but it was quite a few hours at least.

He told me about his exploits and those of his friends.

He made me feel like a human again, not talking to me like I was an animal. When he finally got up to leave, he promised he would try and look in on me again and if I needed anything he would do his best to sort something out.

Again I sat there in silence. It was very quiet outside of the door, no footsteps, no voices; nothing. I had figured out we must be close to some kind of entrance, because previously I had heard the doors slide open and close. I sat and waited for the next session that surely awaited me. Feeling drained both mentally and physically. I closed my eyes, put my feet up on the table and dreamt of being somewhere a million miles away.

Click, click, clunk, the door opened quickly. As soon as I heard the first click I sat bolt upright.

Moonface and Daffy came in for their daily visit. I hated these bastards so much. They sat in their usual spots; Daffy beside me and Moonface behind the desk. He looked at me with a bemused look.

"I have your medicine Alam, it will be here shortly. You have a problem with your chest? Do you smoke?"

"No, it's nothing to do with smoking."

"Why you smoke sheesha?"

"I don't smoke sheesha."

"Mr Alam, I am asking you why you smoke sheesha because on Monday afternoon you were sitting at Hilton Jumeirah and you smoked sheesha with your friends, yes?" His head was tilted to the side clearly puzzled.

"Yes, I did I try it, but I am not a regular smoker."

"If you have bad chest, then why you try?"

"Somebody told me it might be good for the chest and for just relaxing."

I thought back. My brain had been consumed by my

present predicament and so Monday seemed like a lifetime ago. I closed my eyes and let my mind take me back to what was probably only five, or maybe six days earlier. Ah, yes. On Monday, I was at the Hilton with a group of friends who had come over from England for a short break. It was a nice mixed group, as some were with their families and some had come alone. We had all got together and had been drinking freshly squeezed fruit juices, someone had suggested that we should share a sheesha between us. So yes, it was true about my smoking. But how the hell did this lot know about it?

"We have been to Z's apartment …we find something very interesting in your suitcase. So I ask you once again, do you smoke?"

"No I don't smoke, I told you."

"Hmm…………." Moonface squinted his eyes, looking at me in a way that reminded me of the disappointed look my father had when I didn't get an 'A' on some test at school.

"You keep saying you don't smoke, Alam. So why you have thirty cartons of cigarettes in your suitcase?"

I instantly remembered. Oh fuck… the cigarettes. Most of our friends back in England smoke and the price of a single pack of twenty is extortionate to say the least. Here in Dubai we could pretty much buy two hundred for the price of twenty back home, so we had bought some of the cheapest ones we could find, intending to split them between us before leaving and take them home for our friends. Granted, it was quite a lot of cigarettes, but hardly enough to put us into the international cigarette smugglers category.

"I bought them as gifts for friends," I told Moonface.

"Why? Are they cheap?"

"Yes they are much cheaper than in England. One packet of twenty is around five pounds; that's like thirty dirhams. Here, for thirty dirhams you can buy a whole carton."

"I have an idea for you. Instead of giving them to friends, why don't you give them to your sister and tell her to put them under the counter. She sells them, you will make good money. That is a good business for you, what you think?"

He looked at Daffy, they both nodded in agreement.

"Yes it's a good idea. I never think of that before. Thank you."

They both eyed me suspiciously. Maybe they had started to cotton on to my sarcasm.

"Look, I'm here to set up businesses that could potentially earn me millions. Why on earth would I need to con the VAT man out of a couple of hundred pounds?"

Daffy spoke up now, spraying a little less spit this time.

"What have you done wrong this year?"

"I haven't done anything wrong."

"You broke the law."

I thought carefully about what they might be referring to.

"Oh, yes, I was caught speeding in the UK."

"No not in UK, here …in Dubai."

I was absolutely certain I had not broken the law in any shape or form in Dubai.

"No, I have done nothing wrong or illegal here."

"Think, Alam. Think very carefully."

"No, there's nothing I can tell you."

"Ok then, I will tell you. On Tuesday night you went to Karama Hotel. There was a Filipino band playing, you were talking to the girls and you wanted to pay the girls to come back to your hotel with you. Z said you gave the girls 1000 dirham."

It was true that me and Z had gone to Karama Hotel on the Tuesday night to meet Ali, an Iranian friend of his. Ali was a long-time associate of Z's and he owned a bunch of stores in Irani market; so-called because most of the stores were run by Iranians. The area was a maze of stores nearly all dealing with counterfeit goods. You would step into a store and look around at the no-name brands and bric-a-brac on sale; if it was obvious you were just a tourist, one of the assistants would ask you if you wanted to buy a Gucci handbag or Rolex watch. Any interest from you would lead to an invite to the back of the store where a fake wall or partition would be removed to reveal stairs leading up or a back room with countless fake goods on display.

The police would raid these shops every so often, but usually just for showing face and more importantly to pick up their bribes and some gifts for the family. A lot of tourists tended to shop here for a bargain, so it was in everyone's interest to allow the black market trade to continue.

We were meeting with Ali to arrange a shipment of genuine pashmina scarves. Ali invited us along to the hotel as it was near his stores and because it was a fun place to hang out. They have these really crap Filipino bands that do cover versions of rock songs. The bands are so bad, they are very entertaining. The manager was a good friend of Ali's, so halfway through the act the manager had introduced us to the band, as well as most of the dancing girls. We had all talked and had a laugh and generally had a real fun evening, but there was none of the bullshit that Moonface suggested.

And then it dawned on me that if they knew we were at the Hilton Jumeira and then at Karama, maybe they had been following us for days. That got me worrying even more. If we had been followed and observed for a period of days, then surely these people would know that our stories were true and we had no terrorist connections? That we were still being questioned like this was a bad omen that someone was stitching us up.

"No, I did not pay the girls to come back to the hotel. I would never ask the girls improper things."

Daffy butted in, "we can get statements from the girls to the contrary. If you lie, you will be punished."

"You know what? I'm sure you can get statements that say anything. So do it. I would much rather be punished for that, than be accused of the bombing."

"Don't speak to me like that! Tell me Alam; you have a girlfriend?"

"Same answer as yesterday."

"Which is?"

"Yes."

"Is she good?"

"Yes."

Damn this was frustrating. I was finding it hard to keep my temper in check. Despite the fatigue, the hunger and the threat of violence, I wasn't going to let the bastards break me.

"I look at your file. You have son, but you don't live with him and his mother?"

"Yes."

"So you live with girlfriend, but you don't get married?"

"Yes."

"Hummm... you like to fuck Mr Alam? You like to

fuck?"

As he spoke, he stood up grabbed me by the throat and wrenched me up from the chair, putting his face right up close to mine. The stains on his jagged teeth too close for comfort.

"I said you like to fuck, Mr Alam?"

"Not with you," I couldn't stop myself saying.

Suddenly he punched me in the groin, grabbing my testicles hard. He twisted them like he was turning a doorknob. The pain shot through me and I doubled over. I lay on the ground panting like a dog, with my eyes watering and a dull ache in my balls.

"Tum ko garam koon hai? You have hot blood?"

He spoke in Urdu for the first time. It took me a few seconds to realise, as it came out of the blue.

"Tum ko garam koon hai?"

It wasn't very good; it was about on a par with my own grasp of the language. I was still doubled up in pain and just ignored him. Moonface had sat in silence so far, but at this point he left the desk and made for the door.

"Ok. I have tried to help you, Alam. I have been very kind, but my patience wears thin. Now this is it for you. No more nice chat anymore. There are men here who will make you tell the truth. It is time that you met with them."

I was still in a foetal position on the floor when they both left. I had barely had time to catch my breath and wipe my teary eyes, when a guard came in and blindfolded me. Without a word he dragged me back to my cell, removed the blindfold and told me,

"Get your things. Hurry! You have new room."

I couldn't help noticing the sneer when he said 'new room.' All I had was a water bottle and a toothbrush that had been given to me by one of the guards, along with a small bar of soap.

"Come. Come with me."

I stood in front of my guard, expecting to be blindfolded, but instead, he swung me around and pushed me down the corridor, the first time I had been that particular way. If the blindfold had been left off so I could take in exactly where I was going, then these guys were good at their jobs. The passageway we turned into was dark and damp, with mould up the walls and an underlying unpleasant smell. We walked to the end of the corridor and around the corner to the next row of cells. The only one with the door open was the end one. It was half the height of the regular cell doors, so I had to crouch down to enter it. The guard gestured at the open door, so I ducked my head inside. The stench hit me immediately and I paused involuntarily, but my guard pushed me inside, where I landed on the heavily stained mattress that took up most of the space. The guard said something in Arabic. I wasn't sure what it was, but I had heard it said before by Arabic speaking friends and knew it meant something like 'only Allah can save me' or something like that. And with a smile, he slammed the door shut. Complete darkness. I tried to half stand up, but even on my haunches, my head touched the ceiling. The bastards had switched off the air conditioning, leaving me only the stinking stale air to breath. I tried to open the letterbox for the food parcels, but it was shut from the outside. I just about managed to sit up and lean against the wall. This must be what it would be like to be shut in a coffin, to be buried alive. I slumped on the blood and faeces-stained mattress, willing my eyes to adjust to the darkness, but to no avail. Now I had to use all the positive thinking I could muster, just to block out the smell. I couldn't help but retch a couple of times, but knew if I threw up in here it was only going to make things worse. Fortunately, I managed to stop myself.

I closed my eyes, breathed deeply and counted backwards from twenty. I visualized myself at the beach, sitting in the shade, all nice and relaxed. The sun gently warming my skin; a gentle breeze passing every now and again, swaying the palm fronds rhythmically just above my head. And all the time in the background, the gentle sound of the water lapping at the shore of a sun-kissed paradise that was all mine.

Chapter 5
Poisoned Pyjamas

Several sleepless mind numbing hours later
I didn't hear the footsteps and only heard the second click. The guard I had christened 'Skinny' opened the door and beckoned me outside. Without blindfolding me, he pushed me along the passageway to the toilets.

"Strip. Shower. You have two minutes."

I stepped under the so-called shower. The water trickled out in a pathetic manner, changing between lukewarm and blisteringly hot. The guard stood watching me.

"You hurry up, be quick."

I flinched under the scalding water as it burned me. I soaped and rinsed off as quickly as I could, then I stepped out and dried myself with the dirty blood-encrusted towel that was given to me. I wiped off one stink only to replace it with another. A vest and underpants were handed to me.

"Put these on." Skinny said, holding them at arm's length.

They looked utterly disgusting. They were a grimy grey colour that suggested they may have once been white. They were also very crisp and flat, which just made them look like they had been recently ironed, even if not recently washed. I put them on, unable to hide the distasteful look on my face. The underpants were several sizes too big, with the crotch hanging down closer to my knees than to my balls.

Skinny then gave me a set of blue pyjamas and it was instantly apparent that they too were way too big for me. I put them on anyway; Skinny could barely hide his amusement.

"Quickly, come," he said with a smile and off we went again.

I was led back to the cell with my normal clothes in one hand and my other hand holding up my baggy pyjamas. Back in the cell I used my belt to tie around the waist. The guard went off leaving the door slightly ajar. Maybe this was deliberate, they wanted to see me try to escape and then they would have a valid reason to shoot me. Or maybe he just felt sorry for me not having had any light or fresh air? Yeah, that must be it. I shook my head at my own naivety. Nothing happened by chance here. Nobody cared about me. They're just fucking with you, Alam. I looked at the mattress and it really was as disgusting as I had imagined. I pulled the door shut. I would rather be in darkness than sit here looking at this heap of shit.

As I sat there, I felt my temperature was increasing. Not just my forehead or the back of my neck, which was usual. No, it was kind of all over me. Suddenly I was itching like crazy and burning across my lower abdomen. Then it felt like my genitals were burning and my buttocks were on fire too. I felt around in the underwear and there was some kind of powdery substance there, but I couldn't see anything as I had shut the door, there was nothing to get a hold of on my side to open it again. Very soon I was in total agony; scratching and tearing at my skin until a wetness covered my fingers. The bleeding only gave me temporary relief. No matter what I tried, or how much I scratched, nothing could stop the pain

The bastards must have done this deliberately to make me suffer. Well it worked bloody well. Little did I know that I would bleed and itch for over two weeks and no matter how many times I tried to wash it off, whatever it was had firmly embedded itself into my skin.

The door opened slightly and a box was pushed inside before it shut again. I grabbed it and opened it and I could feel some food in there. All I really wanted was a drink, so I was overjoyed to find a carton of juice and drank it down in one gulp. There was also an apple which I wolfed down in a few mighty bites. My belly didn't appreciate the sudden intake and instantly bloated. I didn't want to eat what I couldn't see, so I left the rest.

My accommodation may have changed, but the routine remained the same. By now I had totally lost track of time and when I tried to estimate how long I had been held, I really couldn't narrow it down from between three or four days, to over a week. Every now and then Skinny or another guard would open the door and I would be led away for more questioning. Same questions, same assortment of faces, same threats every time.

"Prepare to die for your cause."

"You will never leave here."

I hate indecisive people. I felt like telling them to hurry up and make up their minds. Is it going to be imprisoned for life or death in the morning?

One time when I was being taken back to my cell, I asked the guard if I could use the toilet. He removed the blindfold and left me to it, telling me to go back to my cell when I was finished. I did what I had to do and was walking back down the corridor when I noticed there was a door open to another cell. It could be Z, or Faz, or Raf! I peered in and saw that there was a working TV. Lucky bastard. Nobody was in the cell so I grabbed the only thing in there, which was a pair of slippers. I was sick of wearing my trainers; I had been wearing them every day for who knows how long. They had become soaked in sweat and reeked like you wouldn't believe. I held the slippers under my pyjama top and walked quickly back to my hell hole.

I sat and waited for the next round, which wasn't too long in coming. Skinny opened the door and beckoned me and I followed him to the end of the corridor where they had set up a fingerprint desk. I was fingerprinted by some miserable bastard who kept trying to break my fingers, he was twisting them one way then the other. Both hands were done, also my palm and the side of my hand, which seemed a bit strange. I've seen plenty of cop shows over the years and had never seen that done before. After this my picture was taken with the obligatory number board and when the photographer nodded at my guard, I was led back to the cell. This time I tried my hardest to sleep. Exhaustion more mental than anything was really setting in…

Don't Worry; Be Happy

I recalled a conversation I had with my mother some months ago. There had been an article in the newspaper about a woman that had four grown-up sons, all in their twenties or thirties, who had all died in various circumstances. Two in different car accidents, one had drowned whilst on holiday with his new wife and the other one I couldn't recall. My mother had expressed that there could be no greater pain for a mother than to outlive her children and for her it would be worse than any hell.

My mother was born in India near Kashmir; her parents having moved there three years earlier from Malaysia. Her father had been a successful merchant having learnt the trade from his father dealing primarily in spices and silk. Mum never told me why they relocated to India, as the country was in the process of becoming partitioned at the time and was going through a great deal of turmoil. She talked about her very privileged lifestyle, about her five sisters and one brother who was doted on by everyone. They had servants who would see to their every need and for a long time, life was good.

When the great partition was finalised, the family found themselves living in what was now Pakistan. This area of Kashmir has been disputed territory ever since and from day one there was a lot of trouble and violence in the area. But the family just went about their business as normal, hoping to keep their heads down and just carry on as before. My granddads business and relative wealth was well known in the local villages and surrounding areas and unfortunately that news eventually spread to the bandits who came to the house one day and rounded up all the children. Mum and her sisters witnessed their father beaten to within an inch of his life; all his money, gold and anything of value was taken from him and he was left for dead. He eventually recovered but life was never the same again. He went back to work but never achieved the success he had previously. Mum finished her schooling, learnt her home skills and did the best she could to help the family get back the lifestyle they had previously known. Eventually it was suggested that she marry her former neighbour, who had left the village to go to England many years before. Mum could barely remember him, but she accepted anyway. Unknown to anyone, my father had already been married and then divorced. He had five children from this marriage, including four boys and they all lived in the same house, along with his ex-wife who had not moved out yet.

By the time I was born, the ex-wife had moved out along with the kids and life had improved dramatically for my mother. My sister followed me little more than a year later, then my brother three years after that and finally another sister a little later.

This tough start in life - both in India and in England - has made my mother the strong woman she is today. Barely 5 foot 2 tall and slightly overweight, she has a warm and very friendly demeanour. The jet black hair has started greying around the edges, but her eyes still sparkle in her round soft face. She has been ill for some time, the pain is etched across her face. She was strong enough to survive a heart attack and travel by plane before she got a medical prognosis. From a young age I was always encouraged by mum to do what I wanted and to believe in myself. She always told me I could do anything and no matter what childhood dreams I shared with her, she always said that if you really want it you can have it.

From the age of four I would accompany mum everywhere, translating and looking out for her. Dad worked a lot of hours, so all hospital visits and trips to the social were taken care of by me. We moved to London in '79, my dad set up a retail store with a small wholesale operation attached. During my school years I would help out early mornings and straight after school. Up until 1987 my family ran the business and did quite well, but then my father had an accident that resulted in him being unable to work anymore, so we sold up and moved back to Huddersfield.

When dad passed away in 1993 I was by default, head of the family. Whenever mum talked about my childhood she was always apologising to me and would often cry saying she was sorry and sad that I didn't have a normal childhood, always burdened with responsibility in one form or another. I didn't see it as being anything other than what it was. Whenever there were problems, mums motto was don't worry; be happy.

All that pain she had through her life, I didn't want her thinking her son had done her or the family wrong or let her down in any way. The bond with her was so strong, I only had to walk in the room and she would know what was on my mind. Many times she would say she had a feeling or dream that I was unhappy or worried and mostly she was right. For the first time since my incarceration, I sent her prayers and love, knowing that if she heard me, then she would not believe whatever lies may be said about me.

A couple of hours passed, spent thinking about home, my family and what I could have done to deserve this treatment. As I lay there half-awake, half daydreaming, I didn't notice the door open. The first I realised there was someone in the room was when I was grabbed by the arm and literally dragged outside. I was blindfolded and cuffed and just thought 'off we go again' as we walked along the now familiar path to the interrogation room. But no, this time we turned right after going through the second gate, instead of left. I was walked through the sliding doors that I'd heard going 'shush shush' the other day, or was it night? Or whatever. At least my hearing wasn't letting me down. Little things like that feel like tiny victories in such circumstances. Immediately through the door, the hot night air filled my nostrils. I took several deep breathes, savouring the freshness. After the stifling heat of my cell, the warmth of the evening covered me like a comfort blanket and despite my hunger and fatigue, I felt strangely exhilarated. I was led down some steps and pushed towards a car with its engine already humming. My head was pushed downwards and I was thrown onto the back seat. The guard then reached inside and pulled a hood over my head, which considering I was already blindfolded, seemed a bit of overkill. Someone got in beside me, the door on the other side creaked open and I found myself sandwiched between two smelly men. Then the front doors opened and quickly slammed shut and I thought, 'Ok, this is it. This is where the real pain is going to start.'

The car roared off at speed, with Arabic music playing loudly on the cheap tinny radio. The car absolutely stank of petrol fumes when I first got in; I was hoping my hood would act as a filter, but that wasn't working, so I tried to bury my head into my shoulder. The car swung in a long arc, sped up for a short time, then braked hard. The engine was switched off and I felt both of my escorts get out. A hand reached in and grabbed my cuffs and yanked me painfully out of the car. I was pulled along like a reluctant dog on a lead, all the time thinking we could have walked here in little more than five minutes, why did we come by car? I walked and stumbled along, went up five steps, through a set of sliding doors and into a room where the AC was set so high, I immediately shivered. I was taken into another room where my hood, blindfold and cuffs were removed. My orders were simple.

"Wait there. Stand still. Do not move."

I looked around the room my eyes adjusting to the brightness. Directly in front of me was a massive mahogany desk, beautifully made with exquisite carved legs and completely out of place in a room such as this. There were two flat screen computer monitors, a keyboard and masses of wires on the desk. And then I noticed the extra thick, heavy-duty cables running across the desk, along the floor and into the chair. The rest of the room didn't matter anymore; my focus was entirely on the cables. I shit myself. I am not ashamed to admit that I did literally shit myself. I am going to be electrocuted to a crisp. I was scared at the pain that was about to be inflicted upon me and I wondered just how much would I endure before passing out or dropping dead. I wondered if I would cry out like a coward begging for mercy, or just sizzle in silence as my brain fried.

A short time later, as I still pondered what awaited me, a man who looked like an Army Officer strode in confidently and motioned towards the chair.

"Please sit down. Salaam. How are you?"

"I've been better," I said, my crackly voice hinting at my unease.

The Officer was a tall skinny man with a slight beard, wearing a pair of trendy glasses that seemed somehow out of place. He had the looks of a nerdy bookworm and in any other situation would not appear scary at all. I realised he was probably one of those kids who was picked on at school and had decided he would torture people to make up for his unhappy childhood.

"I am Major Abdullah," he declared loudly. He only looked about thirty at the most, so how could he be a Major?

"I want to help. Please relax; you look scared," he said in a soft voice.

I smiled nervously, trying my hardest to maintain my composure. Whatever he had in store for me, I would try and be a man.

"Do you know what all this equipment is?" he said matter-of-factly.

"I think you are going to electrocute me."

He laughed, "No, no Alam. What you think we are? Like the Israeli's? No, no. This is a polygraph machine; a lie detector. I have been using this for many years."

"Ok," I said, not doing too good a job of hiding my relief. "Then your machine can tell you I am innocent and I can go."

"Yes, I think you are telling the truth. You look honest person to me, so let's get this done then we can go home. Please relax. Have a drink."

He opened a compartment in the front of the huge desk and took out a carafe and a small glass. He filled the glass with water and passed it to me.

"I will ask you very simple questions, the machine will record the answers. I will ask you easy questions to start with, so the machine can read how you react. Then I ask the real questions, Ok? So, please relax, I want to help you. Just think of me as your friend and we are just talking over some tea. First off, I have to attach some sensors to you, Ok?"

A thick black cable was placed around my chest, just where it meets my stomach on the solar plexus. Then a sensor was placed on my index finger.

"There, not so bad. It is not uncomfortable is it?"

"No, it's fine." I wiped my sweaty palms across my pyjamas and did my best to relax my breathing to somewhere near normal.

"If you are comfortable, I will begin."

"Ok."

I just wanted it over and done with so I could prove my innocence and get the hell out of there.

"You have to give me simple yes and no answers, Ok?"

"Ok."

"Are you Alam Ghafoor?"

"Yes."

"Please sit still, Alam. Don't move around; just focus your eyes on one spot." He pointed to a spot on the floor.

"Do you have a driving license?"

"Yes."

"Do you live in London?"

"No."

"Do you have three sisters?"

"No."

"Have you broken the law?"

"No."

"Do you love your mother?"

"Of course!"

"Yes or no, Alam. Do you love your mother?"

"Yes."

"Ok, that's it. The computer knows how you respond, everything is taken into consideration; breathing and perspiration adjusted for. This is 100 % accurate."

I nodded, but thought I have seen enough TV programs to know it is not fool proof. Anyway it's not like I have to beat the machine; I just tell you the truth. They will soon see that this is a big misunderstanding and I can go home.

"Ok, now I ask you the most important questions. Let's go through them first, so you are clear what I am asking about."

He went over all the allegations that had been already put to me and then started.

"Was your phone used to contact any of the London bombers?"

My breathing was controlled. I stared straight ahead, trying not to sweat too much.

"No."

"Did you know about the plans to bomb London?"

"No."

"Are you Alam Ghafoor?"

"Yes."

"Do you live in England?"

"Yes."

"Did you plan the London bombing?"

"No."

"Did you arrange equipment and funds for the London bombing?"

"No."

"Have you met any of the bombers?"

"No."

And that was the end. Without another word, he whipped the wires off me, slammed the lid of the laptop computer and almost ran out of the room. I sat there wondering if it was all over now? Would I be set free? The same guard as before came in; put on my blindfold and cuffs, then led me back outside to the car. Oh it was so good to breathe the fresh air again, even for those precious few seconds. We made the same journey as earlier, but this time in reverse; accelerate for a minute or so, make a big swinging arc, slam on the brakes. Seconds later I was dragged from the backseat, pulled up the steps, through the sliding door and led back to the cell. Back to the blackness. Back to silence.

****

Raf
—

The cell door opened and a guard came in and half pulled me to my feet. He manhandled me outside and pushed me to the end of the corridor, where a table was set up. My fingers were inked up and papers laid out ready for finger printing. However there was a slight problem; I was sweating profusely. As well as having been stuck in my cell without any air conditioning, I still hadn't had my diabetic medication. Because of these two factors, the ink was not taking to my fingers at all and the guard thought I had deliberately done something so my fingerprints couldn't be read. He became very aggressive and slapped me hard around the head, shook me about and swore at me. I tried to explain that it wasn't my fault, I just needed my medicine; but the guard and the fingerprint man just ignored me.

He inked up the rest of my hand and palm and took a print as best as he could. Then the guard marched me back to my cell and threw me inside.

He returned much later, blindfolded me and led me outside to an already running car. I was driven a short distance to another building and led into a new room. My blindfold was removed and I couldn't believe what I saw; a mass of wires everywhere, thick cables and a couple of computers.

An Army Major entered and introduced himself as Major Abdullah, explaining that I was about to me polygraphed. He explained that he wanted to help me clear up the misunderstanding so I could go home. I went through the questions and answered them all honestly. When it was over, the Major left and I was taken in the car, back to the first building.

Several hours passed until I was taken from my cell once more. No blindfold or cuffs this time. I was escorted down numerous passages until we reached our destination. The door had a guard outside, who went inside to announce our arrival. He then opened the door again and gestured for me to enter. Sat behind an ornate desk was Major Abdullah.

"Ah, Raf. You should know that your friends are gone. They told the truth, that you are the one connected with the bomb blasts. You had your opportunity to tell the truth. You have no more chances."

I was numb. My mind was blank and I could think of nothing to say. The Major stared me down and I averted my eyes, as they started to fill with tears. The guard blindfolded and cuffed me and I was taken for a short car ride to what would be my new accommodation for the next five days.

****

Z

After my little excursion to the apartment, I had been driven back to the same building and thrown in the same cell. I was pretty much forgotten about most of the day, apart from a quick trip to be fingerprinted. Just when I thought I might be left alone to maybe get some sleep, I was beckoned outside by a guard, who blindfolded and cuffed me. I was led outside to a waiting car and after an extremely short ride, I was in another room in another building, facing a man who introduced himself as Major Abdullah. He explained that I was to be polygraphed and that he wanted to help me in clearing up the misunderstanding.

I answered all the questions truthfully, then I was blindfolded and cuffed and thrown back into the car. Shortly after getting back to my cell, the guard came for me yet again and took me to another room where I was surprised to see Major Abdullah was waiting for me. He explained that everybody else had been released, that I was the guilty one and there was nothing more he could do.

****

Alam

In came the guard to put on my blindfold and cuffs. I was then taken for a short ride and into a new room similar to the one where the polygraph had taken place. I was given the order to stand in the middle of the room with my arms in the air. I wasn't in the cell long before the skinny guard came for me again. I was taken to my usual interrogation room and told to stand away from the wall. The Major came in and pulled the two chairs close together.

"Please sit."

He looked pensive, staring at the wall behind me, unable to look me in the eye at any time. He spoke deliberately and slowly.

"Alam, I really wanted to help you and believe you, but you have lied. My machine has told me; never in twenty years have I seen such a clear cut result. Never.

You are the only one who lied; your friends all passed. They have all gone home now."

Tears rolled down my cheeks. The frustration and the fact that I knew he was blatantly lying, by the one sided shoulder twitch.

"No! Your machine is wrong, I haven't lied about anything. Please, if you check with the British Police I have never done anything wrong. I don't have a criminal record, how can you accuse of me this?"

"There was one specific question you lied about. You said you had no contact with the bombers, but we know that you did."

All the time he was talking, he never once looked me in the eye. The lying son of a bitch, I couldn't have failed the machine unless … unless he manipulated it to produce a false reading on purpose, to justify my incarceration to the British Government.

"I have done all I can, it is out of my hands now."

The Major left me sitting there, alone with my thoughts. I fully expected Skinny to come in and take me back to my cell, but he never came in. I just sat there, going through what the Major had said, questioning my own brain. Maybe subconsciously there was some information lodged in my head and that is why the machine reading said I was lying. I nearly convinced myself that somehow, somewhere I must know more than I thought.

Mr Sudan and Mr Fat man came in shortly after. Fatty started speaking,

"Alam, you have lied to everybody. You are involved, now we are certain. Major Abdullah is the best at finding the truth, so tell me, why have you lied?"

"I haven't lied; I am telling you the truth."

"So you say the Major is a liar?"

"No, I didn't say he is a liar."

"You think our machine is wrong?"

"No, your machine is not wrong." I wanted so badly to say yes your bloody machine and your Major are both fucking liars. I was so angry.

"Why did you lie?" He swivelled in the chair side to side.

"I have not lied. Look, everyone knows these machines are not fool proof. There are limitations to their use, that's why nobody can rely on them 100%"

"Oh, so you know about these machines? Maybe you have trained yourself to beat them. But you cannot beat ours," he said with a sneer.

"I was nervous. I was scared because I thought it was an electric shock machine and maybe that altered the reading."

"The machine can take everything into account. You know that we know your friends are innocent; we let them go. You are the bad one…. the evil man."

"No, I am not bad or evil. Please believe me, your results are wrong."

"Enough, Alam. No more lies. I want to know the truth."

The door opened and a new face came in. There was an exchange of words and Fatty got out of the chair and stood against the back wall. This new character sat down in front of me and pulled the chair up so close that I could feel his breath on me. He positioned himself so that his knees were either side of mine. It's a classic position a lot of police use to intimidate subjects being questioned. The invasion of your personal space leads to a breakdown in your self-assurance. We don't like people invading our personal space unless we are on intimate terms with them.

He had a brown wizened worn-out face with a scar running from his right eye down to his mouth. Somebody must have slashed him real good. Whoever had done it had left him with a hard, evil looking face that only a mother could love. He spoke slowly in Arabic, with a soft rhythmic voice. Surely everyone knew by now that I barely could string two words together in their language? His breath stank; an unpleasant mix of stale tobacco and strong coffee.

Fatty, who was stood to the side, explained that this was the most senior man in this complex. After my results had been processed, he had been woken up because of the seriousness of their implications and so he was in a very bad mood.

Again he spoke in Arabic and Fatty translated for me in his broken version of English.

"You better start talking, saying truth this time. We are not going to play games with you anymore. Are you willing to die to protect the others involved with you? Are you willing to die for your cause?"

I was angry and frustrated. I was going round and round in circles with these people. I knew I was innocent; there could be nothing to prove otherwise. They had polygraphed me, they had observed me for days prior to them kidnapping me, so what more could I say or do. I put my open hands up to emphasise to Fatty what I was saying.

"I am not lying. I have told you the truth about everything from the moment you picked me up. All this time you are wasting with me, when you could be capturing real criminals!"

My hands up, my palms towards Scarface, in the

classical 'nothing to hide, nothing up my sleeves' pose. Scarface immediately smacked my hands away and grabbed me by the throat.

"How dare you put your hands up to me," he said in perfect English. "You do not dictate the terms of this interrogation."

"Look, I am trying to explain to you yet again; I haven't done anything and I don't know anything."

He let go of my throat and gave me a good backhand. Then he put his face right up close to mine so that our noses were almost touching. Slowly he stood up without taking his eyes off me, then he and Fatty left together. Mr Sudan shuffled his papers, shook his head and sighed loudly, which I am sure was for my benefit, then he too got up and left me alone with my thoughts. Another new face came a while later and handed me a small box.

"Here, have a drink. Eat some fruit."

He sat at the desk and watched me as I gulped down the fruit juice. It was a little warm and very sweet, but it tasted like nectar to me.

"Alam, why have you lied to us? Why do you still lie? The machine is telling us you lie."

"I don't care what your machine is telling you," I said with a mouthful of apple. The juice ran down my chin as I spoke. "I am telling you the same as everyone else; I have told you the truth all along."

"Alam, I cannot think that after twenty years Major Abdullah does not know how to do his job properly. Do you think he is a liar?"

"No, nobody is a liar, everybody is telling the truth."

"Do you want me to give you a second chance, Alam? Maybe the result will be different."

"If you want to give me a second chance, then yes it is

possible the result will be different second time around."

"This machine is very precise and very expensive. It has never been wrong before. If my brother was questioned by me and tell me something but the machine says he lied, what do you think I should do?"

"I don't know. He is your brother."

"Yes, but if he lied and the machine proved it? I would believe the machine. If it told me he was lying, my own brother could not hide truth from me."

"Maybe, but I am telling you that I told the truth and somewhere there is a mix up. I don't care about your brother or your machine or about the Major. You tell me this; if I have lied and you think your machine is truthful, then hand me over to the British government. Let them deal with me if I have done something against them."

I was angry; so fucking angry. This bullshit was going on and on and I was sick and tired of spouting the same lines over and over to a seemingly endless number of guys. Each supposedly higher in rank or more senior than the one before.

"Hand me over to the British government. Give them your results and let them deal with me. I can't be held here for a crime you say I committed in England."

"I can't do that," he said with a smile that desperately was trying to appear friendly. "You are my brother, they will kill you soon as they have you in their possession," he motioned a slice across the throat. "I want to help you, not kill you." His head shook

Exasperated, I shouted at the top of my voice, "I don't want your fucking help! Let them kill me. I'd rather die in England than here in this dump. I hate it here. I hate it, you and your country! Call the Embassy, call the government. Do whatever it is you have to do."

My voice had faded to little more than a strangled rasp. It was like the sudden explosion of anger had sapped the last of my strength. I slumped into my chair, panting like a dog. My captor just sat looking at me, occasionally moving his head from side to side, like he was mulling something over in his mind. He waited until my breathing slowed down to something resembling normal, then he spoke,

"I cannot do that. I really want to believe you, so I will try and give you a second chance. I hope you will give a good result this time."

Alone again. Tired, angry and increasingly frustrated at this never-ending cycle. I had been raised to believe that if you are honest, then even if there is a misunderstanding, maybe even one as huge as this one, the truth will eventually prevail. I had also been brought up to believe in justice, but had seen no signs of it so far in this hellhole. I had a horrible feeling that had started as a tiny twinge in the depths of my stomach, but now felt like a raging thunderstorm. That feeling was that my fate had already been decided for me. I had been chosen, for god knows what reason, to take the fall on this one and nothing I could say or do was going to change anything. They were going to break me eventually, so I would confess to the heinous acts they were accusing me of instigating. I figured they were lying to me about the others, I doubted if they had let my friends go and they probably just said it in order to frighten me further. They needn't have bothered. A terrible realisation dawned that I was at the point of giving up. Every thought I had was a negative one. Suppose the Embassy had already been informed? They probably couldn't care less; we were just a bunch of ordinary guys trying to run regular businesses.

In the grand scheme of things we were nobodies and more than likely expendable. Just numbers nothing more.

Skinny came in and made an 'up, up' gesture with his hand. I knew the drill by now, so I stood up, stuck my hands out and on went the cuffs. I spun round so he could put the blindfold back on and was led back outside to the sliding doors and pushed across the rough ground to the awaiting car.

When you are in a situation like this, bound and blindfolded, your senses become remarkably acute. I envisioned every turn the car made, felt every little rut and bump we drove over. By now, after a couple of these journeys, I could almost predict when we accelerated, turned and slid to a halt. I was dragged out yet again and led up the stone stairs into the building. I started heading to the left, the way back to my cell.

"No! This way," my escort said, dragging me the other way. He pushed me down the corridor and into a new room.

"Stop!"

The blindfold was taken off me and my eyes squinted in the bright light of this new location.

"Stand over there, away from wall," he screamed. "Hands up, don't move."

I hoped this guard that I hadn't seen before was just new and enthusiastic and wasn't symptomatic of a new harsher approach by my captors.

The door slammed shut with the familiar click, click, clunk and off went the footsteps into the distance. This room was icy cold, with the air conditioning going off full blast. I stood there with my arms stretched out above my head, but it wasn't long before they were hurting. I dropped them an inch or so. I thought I heard noises, so I straightened them as best I could, but it was agony. My back was going into spasms, the muscles screaming with pain and my knees started wobbling. I dared to look around the large room and saw that at the far end there was an imposing ornate desk complete with two flat screen monitors. A very large executive chair behind it and a secretary chair in front, but there were no signs of the cables I'd seen previously. So, no polygraph in here then. It was different to the other room I'd been in, this was much much bigger, there was enough room for four large corner units, with the top sections made of glass, the bottom part all wood. It looked like good quality hardwood, not the cheap mdf units you find at your local DIY store.

The room was quite grand overall, a bit like a stateroom in a big country house. The deep blue carpet was a luxurious thick pile; it felt nice under my feet, as I'd kicked off my slippers at this point. There were ornate drapes and several paintings on the walls. Quite out of place, considering what goes on here, I thought. Looking down on me there were several very large halogen spotlights embedded deep in the ceiling, which explained the extra brightness. I could see the air vent for the AC and noticed the ceiling had large polystyrene tiles. There were no mirrors anywhere and I couldn't see any obvious cameras. Still, I didn't want to put my arms down in case it created more trouble for me, but the pain and numbness was getting too much to bear. So I gingerly put my arms down and shook them vigorously for a minute or so, to restore the circulation then put them straight back up. The time went by slowly. It was hours before I heard footsteps coming my way. The door opened and Skinny came in with a box. Stupidly, I smiled at the familiar face.

"You can sit and eat, but when you finish, you stand up Ok?"

I sat down and opened the box. A slice of processed cheese greeted me along with two slices of bread, a banana and a small carton of guava juice. I sipped the juice and nibbled the banana. I had managed to get by with next to nothing for the last couple of days, so decided I would have a partial hunger strike. Why? I didn't know. But it was something that I could control. Something to do on my terms.

I sat and relaxed as best I could, savouring the fruit juice fighting the urge to gulp it down. I stood up and started walking around the room, trying to maximise the distance by walking along the periphery. I examined the corner units very closely and saw that in all four, the glass section had a lens with a black cloth draped across it. They were probably watching me. I hurried back to my position and put my arms up in the air.

Chapter 6
Pinky and Perky

<u>Sunday 24th July</u>

Skinny came and took the box away. I asked him what day and time it was, 8.30 in the morning he told me. Sunday morning.

"Please can I use the toilet?"

"Wait."

He went off and returned a few minutes later with a blindfold. He walked me down the corridor, to yet another new part of the building. To my left a sliding door whooshed open as we passed, but there were no other gates or barriers until we reached the bathroom.

Skinny removed my blindfold and nudged me into the cubicle. I hadn't needed the toilet; I just needed to find out about my new surroundings. I sat down and listened, hoping to hear something; anything. I didn't know what. I couldn't work out where Skinny was, so I flushed the toilet, came out and washed my hands. Glancing up I caught sight of him behind me in the mirror. I walked over to the hand dryer and just a little more to my left was a window. I looked carefully over my shoulder to see if Skinny was watching me, fortunately he was preoccupied. I peeked through the window. There was a pile of rubble outside that partially obscured the view, but I could see that it was not an enclosed space like the last view of the outside I'd had in my original cell. The roof was not too high and nobody appeared to be guarding the back of it. I gently tried the window, my heart beating fast; I was scared it might make too much noise. I heard footsteps behind me and slid back towards the sink.

"Ok, that will do. Come." Skinny said. The tone was the same as before. He hadn't seen me try the window. He turned me around and reapplied my blindfold. We retraced our steps, me counting them out in my head so that I knew when we were at door of the grand room with the bright lights.

"Stand there. Arms up. No sitting. Ok?"

Time passed slowly, every minute was excruciating. Now I was aware of the hidden cameras I thought I should at least make an effort to do as I was commanded. When the pain became too much I would drop my arms and shake them about to get the blood pumping again.

Fatty came in, he looked at me standing there with my arms in the air and said,

"Mazah atta heh? You enjoy yourself, yes?"

"No."

"You don't like it? We give you nice food, you don't eat. We give you this nice room you don't like. You are fussy man. That is the word?"

"This room is not nice. I am very tired, so why don't you give me a bed? This isn't exactly five star liked I'm used to." He didn't like my cheek.

"This is the best you will have!" Fatty shouted, all red cheeks and bluster. "Soon it will be very bad for you. You have had time to think, I want to know everything. Put your arms down now. Talk."

So I explained yet again how everything I knew about the bombings was from the TV news channels or the newspapers.

"You know the bombers, yes?"

"No I don't know anybody, I told you."

"We know you know the bombers. What did you say to Z when the pictures were first shown on TV?"

"I didn't say anything specifically to Z. I remember I was surprised when the news said they were all from Leeds and Dewsbury. All I said was that some of them are from an area quite close to where my son lives."

"You said you know the bombers. On the telephone you speak with a woman and she told you don't come home it is dangerous, they are looking for you."

"No, no, she never said that! She told me the Police were searching the area where my son lives. She told me to get out of the Middle East because it is dangerous; that is what she said. Nothing about anyone looking for me."

"No you are lying. You told Z you know the bombers when the pictures were on TV."

I thought back to that time. God, how long ago now? Two weeks? Three maybe? If I had been allowed to sleep properly and questioned in a more humane way, I might be able to think more clearly.

"Look, I can't remember the exact conversation we had. Maybe I said I might possibly recognise the face from one of my visits to my son. The paper said one of them had been working at the fish and chip shop, I had been there with my son on many occasions, so it was possible I may have seen him, but I never spoke to him."

"Why have you lied all the time, Alam. You said you don't know the bombers, now you say that you do. The machine was right heh?"

With that, Fatty left. He stopped at the door and said, "Now get your hands back up. Now we have some truth. Someone new will come to see you."

I stood there in disbelief. These fucking idiots are twisting what I'm telling them. He had made it sound and probably convinced himself, that I knew more than I was saying and he had made some kind of breakthrough. I thought back to the test and figured maybe when the question was asked 'do you know the bombers' my subconscious registered the fact that I did know one of them by sight. At least that would or could explain why my result indicated I was lying.

Pinky and Perky were my next two visitors. So these must be the next in line; the guys Fatty had hinted at. They didn't look so scary. They both were tall skinny gangly limbed guys, probably early to mid-twenties. Their facial hair was slight as if they had just hit puberty and grown their first thin, willowy moustaches.

Pinky had a bloodshot eye, his left one and a rather out of place effeminate way about him. Perky had sharper features; a pointed nose and chin and a rather aggressive manner. Much to my dismay.

They had brought another chair into the room with them. Perky sat down in the fancy executive one behind the desk. He kind of squirmed and fidgeted for a while, reminding me of a cat settling itself on a comfy bed. Pinky sat next to him on the chair he had brought in and slammed down a thick wad of papers on the desk. They both motioned me to come and sit on the chair in front of the desk. Pinky spoke in Arabic, I shook my head.

"I only speak English."

Perky snapped at his comrade, it sounded as if he was telling him off. Power struggle between these two. I tried my hardest not to smile.

"What is your name?"

"Where do you live?"

"What languages?"

All the usual questions, all the same answers. I couldn't help tutting and looking bored. Pinky scribbled down everything, I'm guessing that included my bad attitude.

"You have it all in front of you, so why don't you read what I said to your friends and save your breath. Why you keep asking the same questions? It's fucking pathetic."

Perky stood up quickly and motioned to slap me. I didn't flinch.

"Speak with respect. I will ask you what I want."

I apologised reluctantly in my most sarcastic voice. Maybe not a real good idea under the circumstances, but I don't think these guys understood sarcasm, so they didn't notice.

"Anna? Who is Anna?"

"That's my son's mother."

"Your wife?"

"No, she used to be my girlfriend."

"Your girlfriend. And you have baby with her?"

"Yes."

"So she is your girlfriend and you live together."

"No, I live with somebody else, Vicky."

"Oh, Vicky is your girlfriend now. So, you have two girls heh?" he grinned, a lecherous grin. Pinky looked up, all wide-eyed as if in awe.

"No, I have one."

"Ok, so this Anna. You phone her......"

He looked at his papers, flipping a couple of pages.

"Yes, you phone her and she said to you 'don't come

back it is dangerous' That is correct?"

"No," I said as if talking to a child, "she said I should come back as it is dangerous here in Dubai. Looks like she was right, too," I couldn't help adding.

"Why she say that, it is not dangerous here."

"She had seen on the news all the bombs going off in Iraq and Saudi. To her it is all the same."

"You lied to everybody, Alam. But the machine, you could not fool it."

"For fucks sake, how many times are we going to over this!" I shouted in frustration. "I work hard to provide for my family. I have only ever been to Leeds to pick my son up. I am not a terrorist; I have never met these people or been to the mosque or any meeting these people have been to."

"Your family, they have a store?" Perky continued, completely ignoring my outburst.

"Yes."

"It is good business?"

"Yes, I think so. It keeps us all working together and gives us a living. Before my father died, he said he wanted us to work together and look after one another and that's what we do."

"Everything is good, yes. You have no trouble."

"We were robbed once, that wasn't very pleasant."

"What happened?"

"Some guys came into the store and pulled a gun on my sister and brother. They threatened to shoot them if they didn't open the cash register. They robbed all our money."

"What did you think?"

"I was angry that they put a gun to my nephews head. He was only about a year old at the time."

"What happened?"

"The Police are not very good. They never caught them."

"So…you were angry, Alam?"

"Yes."

"Maybe you were very angry."

"Yes I was very angry. The Police are rubbish; they do not find the criminals."

"So, you are very angry….. maybe you want to do something? You are very angry and somebody has to pay. Is that what you felt?"

"Eyyy What ?"

"You are angry, somebody has to pay. You wanted somebody to suffer."

"No hold on. I see where you are going with this. I didn't want to make anybody pay. What you think. I am angry, so I give the order to bomb London? We are in Huddersfield; it is over two hundred miles away and there is nobody in London that I am angry with. You think I am Charlie Bronson in Death Wish 5. This is stupid."

He raised his voice, "you think I am stupid?"

"No, I didn't say you were stupid, I said this idea is stupid. I did not bomb London!"

"Why do you think you are here? Your government told us you come here to hide and to give the orders."

"Not true."

"On the 7th July you went to the Lebanese restaurant at the Dubai marina. You sat with many friends and celebrated after you gave the order for the bombs, yes?"

"No. I was having dinner with my friends because many of them I had not seen for a while. We were not celebrating anything."

"You celebrate because your plan was successful. You

killed many people, Alam."

The hindrance of it all was wearing me down once again. I couldn't summon the anger within, I didn't have the strength. Tears rolled down my cheeks.

"I am innocent. I have a son and a family that I care very much about. I don't want anything to happen to my mother; she had a heart attack before, this stress will kill her."

"It will be your fault."

"Fuck you," I screamed, "it will be your fault! You and all the other jokers here in this fucked up country! Anything happens to her, I'll make you pay!"

"What will you do? You think you can do something." The bastard smirked in a way that fuelled my anger. I shot up out of the chair startling them both. Perky regained composure.

"You want to hit me?" Perky said.

"I want to ....kill you." I spoke deliberately and slowly. "I want to look into your eyes as I choke the life from you. I want your family to feel my pain."

Fear flashed in his eyes and it felt good to hold the upper hand, even for a short time. His face turned away. I was at that point of anger where all you see is black. Rage. How I stopped myself from hitting him, I don't know. I'm not a huge man, but I could have easily snapped both their scrawny little necks before the other guards could come in. I eased back down and stared him in the eye, but Perky wouldn't return my gaze.

"You need time to calm down. We will leave now. You think about what we have discussed. Stand up over there," he said, pointing towards the far wall. "And don't move."

They scurried off, looking nowhere near as cocky as when they had first entered. I was standing in the middle

of the room, thinking, 'I've just about had enough of this.'
What were they going to do to me if I disobeyed? What
new threats could they conjure up? I threw myself onto
the floor and started doing press-ups and sit ups, then I
stood up and did some squats. I carried on until my
muscles cramped and then I started shadow boxing.
Exhausted, I sat on the floor and listened to my breathing.
Footsteps came shuffling along outside, but I just stayed
where I was. The door was opened and a box was handed
to me without a single word. I opened it. Ah, I think it is
food! There were two tubs inside; one filled with a yellow
watery liquid that looked like dishwater and smelled like
it too. The other had a load of badly wilted lettuce leaves.
I drank the liquid. It was lukewarm but just about close
enough to resembling food that I didn't puke. I gave the
lettuce a miss and opened a scrunched up ball of tinfoil
that held three dates. Ok, not so bad. Finally there was a
plastic container like you get with a Chinese takeaway. I
opened it and was shocked to find a lamb chop or
something resembling it and a load of boiled rice with bits
of veg. I took a deep breath, then I gnawed on the bone
like a hungry dog. I tried the rice, but didn't like it. I
finished the meat and washed it down with the small
sealed plastic cup of water. So much for the hunger-strike,
I smiled to myself. Guilty. Rather like a dieter buckling
under pressure when given a chocolate biscuit. When the
guy came to pick up the box, I asked the time.

"2.30."

"Can I use the bathroom?"

"One minute."

Hooded and cuffed. I counted the steps all the way to
the bathroom and all the way back again. I worked out
how many it was to the sliding door. I had a little plan

bubbling away.

As soon as the door locked I started exercising. If I was to get out of here, or even survive in here, I had to be strong. I started walking around the edges of my room and with it being so big I managed a half-decent workout. I took long strides, I took short strides and sometimes I hopped on one leg then the other. I would alternate walking, press-ups, sit ups and squats continuously. Pinky and perky returned later that same day. I was surprised to see them so soon; maybe I could have some more fun with them. As soon as they entered the room Perky spoke up triumphantly.

"So you are paid one million pounds for the bombing."

"What are you talking about?"

"You are paid one million pounds……..yes?"

"No I am not paid anything…I am not the bomber."

He shuffled the papers in front of him.

"You phoned Vicky and you told her a million pounds will go to your account in one or two days. This is fact."

I thought back. Shit… I didn't realise a little white lie would work so badly against me. The original trip to Dubai was intended for ten days, however we were enjoying ourselves so much, we had extended by three days and then on the day before we were due to fly home, we had managed to get the airline to extend our tickets again, taking us up to a full twenty one day trip. We were just a group of guys having a good time; there was nothing sinister at all about the extension. Every time I had spoken with Vicky she had been constantly nagging me as to when was I going to return to the UK. In order to placate her, I had told her that myself and Raf were working on a really big deal, possibly worth over a million pounds. Which we were and the money would be through in a matter of days. These bastards had recorded the phone calls and had come to a very stupid conclusion that this was payment for the carnage in London.

"You met some men at the regency Hyatt. Who were they?"

The way these bastards were twisting everything, I really didn't want to mention any names, especially of friends or acquaintances. I could pretty much guarantee they would find some way to incriminate me, no matter what I said. However...there was a doubt in my mind about two guys we had been introduced to at the meeting in the Grand Hyatt. Mustafa and Karim; two French Algerians or Moroccans, I wasn't quite sure.

Mustafa was in his mid to late twenties. I found him to be friendly and sociable and pretty enjoyable company overall. It would be hard to describe him to anyone as he was average in every way. Clean shaven, medium brown hair, medium build, maybe just a bit taller than myself and with no distinctive features at all. A photo fit of Mustafa would look like half the population of the Middle East.

Karim, on the other hand, was much shorter than his friend and sported an extremely thick beard. He wore dark glasses throughout our meeting and I remember thinking at the time that he was very quiet and shifty looking. I noticed that he was constantly fidgeting about, like he had a nervous tic of some sort that wouldn't let him sit still. And even with his glasses on you could tell that his eyes were darting all over the place, taking in everything, studying everyone who entered the Hotel. One other strange thing was that he never spoke to any of us that day, he always whispered to Mustafa who passed on what he'd said. I thought it strange, because if he only spoke

French, then why the need to whisper? And other than that, I would have thought he would speak Arabic. Still, no-one else seemed bothered by his strangeness, so I ignored it and just let the day play out.

We only met up with these guys because they had been invited along by a good friend of ours called Naj, who lives in Dubai full time. Naj is a French Moroccan, hence the assumption about the other guy's background. I always liked Naj, he was a laid back guy and very successful in real estate, which is how we met in the first place.

During lunch we talked about business and the opportunities in Dubai and the reasons why Mustafa wanted to relocate here. He said he felt France was not a good environment to conduct business, but didn't really explain why and we didn't push him on it. To be honest, I felt a little pissed off at their presence, as the lunch was supposed to be a chance to catch up with Naj, but I supposed that he had invited the other two along as they were in a similar position to us and maybe he thought we could share tips or something. So after lunch we took a stroll around the beautiful gardens. Karim still insisted on whispering everything to Mustafa. He did something on our stroll that seemed more than a little odd to me.

The gardens had a bridge over the artificial lake that was wide enough for several people to walk over together. As we approached the bridge, Karim suddenly stopped and started jabbering away in Mustafa's ear. I couldn't work out if the look on his face was one of anger, or fear. Mustafa enlightened us by stating that there were women coming the other way who were just about to cross the bridge and that we shouldn't cross it until the women were completely clear. He didn't explain the reasoning behind this, or why it was such a big deal to Karim, but the rest of us looked at each other in puzzlement, shrugged our shoulders and waited for them to cross.

After our stroll, we explained that we were going to Ajman that afternoon to register a business name at the trade centre. Around the Emirates there are a number of these trade centres, known as free zones, any business registering within these zones doesn't have to pay the local taxes or have to comply with the usual rules and laws that exist elsewhere. Most businesses are used as intermediaries for transporting luxury goods around the world, saving fortunes on import and export taxes and duties.

Ajman itself is a boring nondescript place, the smallest of the seven Emirates. Apart from the free zone, the only other thing going for it is that it has a liquor store where you can buy without a license. It doesn't open until late afternoon, but the queues build up very quickly with cars coming from all over the UAE and even from neighbouring Saudi Arabia to buy lots of tax-free alcohol.

When we told Naj of our plans, Mustafa asked if he and Karim could come along as they also wanted to register a business. They obviously hadn't looked into how the registration process worked, so when the cost was revealed to him he nearly fell off his chair! It was the only time we heard Karim speak, as the two of them argued in Arabic, which Raf later told me was something about not preparing properly.

We all drove back to the Hilton and when we got there Mustafa put forward a proposition. He asked us to lend him the money for the business license and he would provide us a post-dated cheque. This might sound a bit strange to most people, but in all the Emirates, anybody that issues a post-dated cheque has to honour it by law. If for any reason you renege, you will face immediate imprisonment. No excuses, no second chances. He said that he needed 20,000 dirhams for the license they wanted, if we could lend him that amount, he would write a cheque for that sum, plus another 5,000 as a thank you. We told him that unfortunately we were not in a position to help with such a sum, even if we wanted to. Mustafa was visibly disappointed, I genuinely felt a little sorry for the guy, because if this licence was the sole reason for their visit, it looked like they had wasted their time and money. He said that if we could find some way to help him out, he would add 10,000 to the loan. Talk about dangling a carrot!

We politely told him we would try to arrange some funds, as they were friends of Naj's, but we were doubtful that it would happen. We gave him our number and told him to ring us later that evening and we would give him a definite answer.

My story over, I sat back and waited for Pinky and Perky to start picking it apart. They just stared at me, faces blank as if waiting for me to continue.

"That's it. That's the whole story. If I found them suspicious, surely you do too."

Still they sat in silence. Pinky scribbled in his notebook, then turned and whispered something to Perky. Perky spoke.

"Maybe…they …just ..wanted to set up in business?"

I couldn't believe the disinterest.

"I have just told you these were a couple of suspicious bastards and you're telling me you're not interested? Surely you could twist this into something more…you managed it with everything else I've told you."

"Alam, you are trying to pass the blame to these guys. They are business men. I want to know who is the gang behind all the bombs? Think about it; we will come back and you tell us. Stand up over there. Don't move."

As soon as the door locked I started walking around the edge of the room. Every now and then I would go into my routine of press-ups, sit ups and squats. I kept track of time by the food packages that had started coming in regularly. Breakfast was roughly seven to eight thirty; lunch was between twelve and two and supper sometime between seven and eight thirty.

I paced around the room thinking of happier times. My thoughts always came back to my family; my brothers, sisters, my mum my son. Then on to the relatives who I suspected were jealous of my success. How they would gloat at my predicament, claiming they knew all along that I was up to no good.

I recalled an incident I had read about a couple of months earlier, where a British woman leaving Dubai was accused of tampering with her passport. She had been arrested and when the police asked for a urine sample it was found that she had what are classed as an illegal substance in her bloodstream. The illegal substance was actually a prescribed medication for back pain, legally prescribed by her English doctor, but banned under UAE law. After her doctor's notes were sent over and translated, they were handed to the British consulate, who decided at that point to intervene on her behalf. Eventually she was freed and allowed home, but the whole process took several weeks to be sorted out. Now supposing the British consulate was to intervene on our behalf; how long would it take for us to be freed? You see, I still had a tiny spark of hope that maybe; just maybe we could still get out of this mess.

I threw myself down, did some more press-ups and sit ups then knocked out fifty squats. Feeling tired, I lay on the floor. Every time I thought I heard noises approaching, I would quickly stand up with my arms in the air. When the noises passed, I would sit back down.

If they were watching me.... fuck them.

As regular as clockwork, I guessed around every thirty minutes or so, somebody would open the door, look me up and down, ask my name then tell me the usual command – hands in the air, don't move, don't sleep. Then they would lock the door and go. The hours went by so painfully slow that I was getting bored of my exercise routine, so I changed it around a bit. First off I shadow—boxed and then I practised my salsa; anything to break the boredom. I remember thinking, 'If you're watching this, I hope you like my moves. Can you imagine Osama doing this? Not very Jihadi, eh?'

My interrogators came and went. I saw the usual crowd at different times: Pinky and Perky, Daffy, Moonface, Fatty, Mr Sudan and mini Fat man. Same questions, same answers. Like hells version of Groundhog Day. Finally a new face came in; a guy on his own, with a face that made him come across as stupid. He was so gormless looking. I later named him Gollum. Reasons for which will become clear.

He was soon coming to see me regularly. He would come in and ask me to sit down. Then he would ask me my name, write something down and then just stare at me for hours. Tilting his head one way then the other, squinting his eyes then looking down his nose. Every now and then he would break the silence by uttering a single question; why? I answered him the same as always, then he would say 'tell me something new.'

I wasn't given any breakfast or lunch one day and when the evening meal came, my relief was short-lived as it was the most unappetising dish I'd ever seen. It was some kind of burger, if I had to guess, I would say chicken. A chicken burger without the bun. Stingy bastards. Somebody must be following the Atkins diet. There were a few measly chips; six to be exact. They were half-cooked and slimy and they tasted almost raw. There was a small slice of bread, a wilted salad and dishwater soup again. I ate the burger, a couple of chips and took a sip of the soup. I inspected the salad to see if anything was crawling on it and after all that decided to give it a miss.

Within half an hour of eating, my stomach started rumbling terribly. Not a hunger rumble, or a satisfied 'ate too much but what the hell' rumble; it was more of a 'oh oh, think I may be in trouble 'kind of feeling. The bastards must have poisoned me! What if I died of food poisoning and then they found out I was innocent? Fortunately somebody came along just as the cramps really started kicking in, so I asked to be taken to the toilet. On went the blindfold and cuffs and I practically led my own way to the bathroom. I rushed inside, quickly squatted down and pebble dashed the wall behind me. Pheww, that was close. I felt a sweat break out, so I took my time as I cleaned myself and washed myself down. When I came out, the guard couldn't stop sniggering. Just as I thought, the bastards did something to the food and they all know about it.

Back in my cell I knew I would be left alone until the morning. I was tired, but started walking the room again. I decided to climb on top of the chair and inspect the ceiling. I lifted the tiles, checked the air con system, trying to figure if I could get up in there and crawl outside. I pushed the tile fully up into the space and thought about heaving myself up to see if the frame could support my bodyweight.

Just as I was about to do it, I heard keys jangling outside the door. Shit! I quickly pulled the tile back in place, jumped down and put the chair by the desk, got back to my usual position and put my arms in the air. The door opened. In came Daffy…my heart sank. I despised his partner Moonface and assumed he was following behind him. Fortunately Daffy was alone.

"Alam, please sit down," Daffy said quite politely. He sat behind the grand desk and gently swivelled his chair from side to side.

"Alam…… bollo tum neh kya socha."

"What have I been thinking about?" I answered in English. "I have been thinking about nothing. I have told you everything a hundred times."

"No tum choot boll ta heh."

"I am not lying."

"Socho kush socho."

"Think of something? Look, my Urdu isn't that good. You want me to think of something? You want me to make something up? To lie?"

He stared at me. I stared back. We stayed in this stare-off for several minutes. His phone went off and he was all smiles as he chatted away. I could just about hear the voice on the other end, so I knew he was talking to a lady friend. He rushed out of the room and I could hear him talking excitedly in the corridor. His voice faded as he walked away.

I was left there, sitting in the chair. Well that's what I

was told to do. So I'll stay here, I reasoned. My body felt so tired, I closed my eyes, desperately craving a proper sleep. What little food I'd consumed today had been purged, my whole being ached with hunger and fatigue. I kicked my feet up on the table, tried to relax my body and my mind, but it was an impossible task. The adrenalin had been coursing through my veins ever since we were picked up and sleep just wasn't on the agenda. I closed my eyes, they were dry and sore, so just resting them for a while was comforting. I made myself as comfortable as I could possibly be, but ever conscious of any sounds coming towards my door.

Whatever position I tried just wasn't comfortable for long, so I put my feet back on the floor and tried to prop myself on my left arm and then my right. I heard noises and sat up bolt upright. The door opened and in came Daffy again and sat back behind the desk.

"Bollo alam. Speak."

I didn't say anything, so we resumed staring at each other. Then he adjusted the flat screen monitor in front of him, so he could see his reflection. After adjusting his headdress, he started pouting his lips Mick Jagger style. I wanted to laugh at the ugly bastard admiring himself and sing out " I can't get no satisfaction" but thought better of it. He checked his left profile, then his right, then he smiled at himself. Seemingly happy with what he saw, he turned towards me, the smile disappeared.

"Bollo kuch ta bollo."

"Speak, speak something? Like what?"

"Tum ider bees sall ke lee ay raygay!"

"Twenty years, you say. Wow, that's a long time."

I was tired of their games and didn't feel like playing along. The door opened and Moonface came in. Oh fuck,

I wasn't in the mood for him just now. The bastard unsettled me just by looking at me. He stared at me as he walked in, his eyes burning into me all the time as he grabbed a chair and seated himself next to me. His evil little beady eyes went through me.

"Alam, why don't you give us information?"

"I have told you everything," my weary voice replied.

"No, you have not given us important information."

"How good do you know Mr Rafique and Mr Z?"

"I know them well enough to know that they are not terrorists."

"You don't know everything about them," he said enigmatically.

"They have no extreme views; they have never spoken about anything political in all the time I have known them."

"I am married, Alam. I don't know everything about my wife."

"Your point?"

"If I was with her all the time, I would know where she goes and who she talks to. But I cannot do this, I have to work."

"I see what you are saying. Yeah, maybe your wife is a terrorist."

His lip curled "You do not know everything about these people you call friends. I do not think they are your friends. Just look at where you are because of your friendship," nodding his head in agreement with himself.

I sat quietly, not reacting to his baiting of me. There was no way he was going to turn me against my friends. And anyway, what could I say? I knew they were all innocent.

"You must think. Tell us what you know. Maybe you

have seen something, maybe you are scared to say. Did they threaten you or your family? We can help you if you help yourself."

"I want to speak to my family to tell them I am safe. I want to make sure my mother is Ok."

"You cannot speak to anybody, Alam. If anything happens to your mother or your family, it is because of what you did."

Moonface looked across at Daffy, who was busy admiring himself in the monitor again. He shook his head at such vanity, then turned his attention back to me.

"You must think. Do you want to die here? Do you want to see my face every day for next twenty years? I can give you pain, Alam. Such pain. You will beg me to let you die."

He gestured to Daffy, who got up from behind the desk and together they left. Moonface, the evil bastard. He really had it in for me. I sat in the chair and stared at the monitor. Then an idea struck me, so I got up and looked around behind the desk. There was a keyboard and a few cables, but no tower. So maybe the computers were all networked? I followed a wire and found a little microphone placed in the well of the desk. Maybe they were listening to every interrogation or recording it. I tried the monitors, switching them on and off all to no avail. I was thinking that maybe I could get online and send an email out to somebody, to let them know where I was. I just couldn't get the damn thing to work. I heard noises, so I sat down quickly. Just in time as it happens. The door opened.

"What is your name?"

"Alam."

"Stand up. Hands up. Don't sleep."

The door closed. I waited awhile then started to play around with the computer equipment again. Keep on trying, Alam, I told myself. If it's possible then you will find the way. But no matter what I did the thing just wouldn't work. I finally exhausted every possible combination of switches, wire traces, things to plug in or unplug. Nothing would give me a screen to explore, so I gave up. I sat down and closed my eyes, with one ear listening out for the door. All night we played out the routine of random door knocks and the order of Stand up. Hands up. Do not sleep.

****

Raf

Having spoken with Major Abdullah the previous day, now was the time for me to find out the verdict on my lie detection test. I sat waiting while the Major studied the ream of papers. He looked up and told me,

"Your friends are gone now. They all speak the truth. You have been lying Mr. Siddique, the result is clear. The machine always knows."

He left and somebody else came in and cuffed and blindfolded me, then escorted me out of the building to a waiting car. I was pushed inside and forced prostrate, so I was kind of lying across all the seats, with my head in the footwell. We drove for a short time; a voice gave me a running commentary as we went.

"Keep your head down. You should tell them the truth. You look like a good man; do not protect your friends, only yourself."

After our short journey I was manhandled out of the

car and led into the other building. I found myself in a new room, where the cuffs were taken off me and the blindfold removed. I was ordered to stand in the middle of the room and told not to move. The pins and needles in my arms were causing extreme pain, but I was scared to put my hands down in case they were watching. I endured it best I could, but it had been three days since I had any medication for my diabetes and I was feeling very weak. Two men eventually came in and started questioning me. They asked if I knew that Alam and Z were terrorists. They were especially suspicious about Alam because of some Leeds connection. They pointed out that I had the same name as the guy from Leeds and where I lived was not far from there. I was light-headed and starting to get dizzy. They told me I was not allowed to sleep and frightened me by telling me they could kill me any time they wanted, otherwise they may just keep me as a prisoner forever.

****

Z

I was left standing alone in a room for hours on end. Various different Officers would periodically come into the room to check I was still in position. An officer came into the room and motioned for me to sit down. I asked him the time and he told me it was 12pm Sunday afternoon. Sunday! Only been here four days. He asked me what information I had on the attacks in London. I replied as I had done previously, saying that I knew nothing at all. My concern is for my wife and children who are resident in London and therefore just as much at risk as anybody else. The officer was adamant that I would not be leaving the building until I told them what I knew. I asked for a phone call to the British consulate or my wife or my lawyer, but he just smiled and shook his head. I was subjected to eight hours of questioning with the constant cycle of the same questions over and over again. There must have been a shift change, as another officer came in and continued asking for the same information. This continued through the night, right up until morning prayers.

Chapter 7
Who is the baker?

Monday 25th July

It was breakfast time again. Another, mostly sleepless night gone by. It's funny, because you would think that when the body is exhausted it takes any quiet opportunity to shut down and rest. But that is not the case at all. Despite my fatigue, I found sleep to be fitful and sporadic. I guess that the subconscious mind is continually turning in these kinds of circumstances, making a proper sleep impossible. Even when I thought I may be drifting off, any slight noise would have my eyes wide open in anticipation of a visitor. I opened my morning food box. I drank the juice and ate the processed cheese slice. There was a small plastic container of soggy cornflakes and lukewarm milk. The container had probably been left out in the sun, as the cornflakes tasted vile and when I brought the carton up to my nose, I smelled that it was slightly off. I took that single spoonful and then closed the lid. The guy who dropped off the breakfast came back after twenty minutes or so. He picked up the box and motioned for me to stand in the middle of the room. I waited a while after he left, then I resumed my exercises, doing some press-ups, squats and shadow-boxing. I tried balancing on one leg and then the other for as long as I could, all mixed up with a few yoga poses I'd learned over the years. This really knackered me out, so I sat on the floor waiting for the day to begin. The door opened and in came Fatty and Scarface. I heard them approaching the door and had jumped up, so when they entered I stood tall with my back straight and chest pushed out. They looked at me then Fatty said something in Arabic and they both laughed.

"You are standing very strong. You look strong, but we will break you very soon. Then we will see how you stand. It is going to be very bad for you."

They sat down in their usual positions; one behind the desk, the other up close and personal. Fatty waived his hand at the empty chair by his friend.

"Come sit. So you have nothing new to say?"

"No."

"Tell me who is Bash?"

"My friend in England."

"Has he come to Dubai?"

"He is not here, but he has visited before."

"How you know him?"

"From college many years ago."

"You know what he does."

"Yes he is a lawyer."

"Is he involved with bombs?"

"No, definitely not."

"Are you sure?"

"Yes I am sure."

"Who is the Baker?"

"I don't know any baker's."

"There is somebody who is the Baker."

"I don't know what you are on about."

"Ok, you know who drives taxis. A Mr Kad."

"Kad? Maybe Quadeer? He is Ziggy's brother."

"Who is Ziggy."

"Quadeer's older brother."

"Who is Kad? K A D." He spelled it out.

"Look I only know Quadeer. I have met him a couple of times. I don't know anymore and I don't know a Kad."

Scarface said something in Arabic. Fatty nodded and then for a few moments there was silence. Scarface studied me, looking like he was planning his next move. Then he pulled his chair round from behind the desk to come square on to me. He just stared at me. He grabbed my face and pushed it down, violently twisting my neck.

"Don't look at me. Why do you lie, Alam? Do you know what is going to happen? We have special men who can make life very painful for you."

"They are coming and they will make you talk," Fatty added helpfully. "It will be much better for you to tell us now. These people will not have mercy."

There was a knock at the door. Fatty got up and went outside and for a couple of seconds I could hear him speaking with somebody, but then the voices faded as they walked off down the corridor. Scarface sat there, I could sense he was still staring at me, so I gingerly looked up; keeping my head in the position it had been pushed into. I glanced at him but did not dare to let my eyes meet his directly. He wasn't looking at me anymore; he had leaned towards the desk and adjusted the monitor so it swivelled round to face him. He started adjusting himself in the reflection, playing with his head dress and checking his profile from different angles. I couldn't believe it; these vain bastards they always wanted to check themselves out! We sat in silence until eventually he got up and left.

Lunchtime came and went and again I ate very little. Pinky and Perky turned up after lunch. Perky had a list of phone numbers which he read out to me. I told him the ones I knew and gave him names to match. The numbers were for my home, my sisters and my son and a couple of friends; the rest I wasn't familiar with. They seemed pleased that I had been so forthright and hurried off when the list was finished. Perky returned a little later with a single sheet of paper in his hand. He asked me for the names again, the same as before. He pulled another sheet of paper from his pocket and I could see it was a list of numbers, times and dates. He asked me about my phone calls, particularly to my son, who I called almost every day. He asked me about a particular time at the Hotel when I had gone in the bathroom to make a call. I explained there was Z, Faz and Raf were in the room and I wanted to talk in private to my son. As he spoke, my mind went into overdrive. Surely he would only know about this if the room had been bugged and monitored by cameras. The bastards had been watching us from the time we arrived. Was the Hotel monitored by default? Or was this set up purely for us?

It brought to my mind a conversation I'd had with a Dubai taxi driver once and in light of that chat, things started to make sense. He was moaning about the ever-increasing numbers of CCTV cameras everywhere. He said they were not for the purpose of fighting crime, but more so to watch everybody; constantly recording everything, which was then archived until needed. Should the Police or the authorities need to stitch you up over anything, it was convenient for them to have this setup in place. They could use old footage to say you were seen with a prostitute, or better still, they could break your door down if they were monitoring you real time and saw that you had one in your apartment or hotel room. Even couples on holiday who were not married could be arrested for having what was deemed in Dubai to be an illegal relationship. Taxi drivers and cleaners were told to report back to the Police on a regular basis with information and most of them did just that, their fear of the Police overriding any moral obligation they may have felt for their guests or passengers. He said that most of the hotels had cameras fitted and the guests would never know. When he told me all this, I presumed that the lobby, the restaurant and any open and public place would have cameras, I mean that's par for the course everywhere these days. But I didn't think they could have them in the rooms, but then as the conversation with my interrogator was proving, that was naive on my part.

I asked Perky if he had any children and when he shook his head, I told him when you and your wife do, you will understand the bond a father has with his child. He told me that he had married his childhood sweetheart. She had moved away with her family, when she was young and he had been heartbroken. But ten years later, he had met her again and the feelings were still there for both of them and they had gotten married as quickly as possible. Inshallah, soon they would start their own family. It felt like we were having a normal conversation. I talked more about my son and I could see he was touched. I wanted to let him know I was a normal guy with normal problems, not some crazed bomber. I'm sure he could feel my emotions and could tell that I spoke from the heart. He smiled at me, the friendliest smile I'd seen in four or five days and I'm sure he was glassy-eyed as he patted me on the shoulder and left the room.

Gollum turned up later that day, bringing me my evening meal. He sat down and ignored me as I went through the box, picking out the drink and a few dates. He waited until I closed the lid and then he started with the usual round of questions. He was playing with his phone all the time he was talking to me and I could see that he had a Lord of the Rings screensaver. I asked him,

"That is your favourite film?"

"Yes I like it."

"I don't understand it. What makes it so good?"

In his broken English and with a stupid grin, he said, "Ohh, it is very good. Special effects. Goblins," he added with a schoolboy's enthusiasm.

We talked about it for a while and to be honest I was asking any old shit, just to break the monotony of the questioning. I thought I should fuck with him, just to relieve the boredom.

"I know why you like it so much; I think it's because you look a lot like Gollum!"

He flipped out majorly.

"What? What you say? You think you can sit here and joke with me? I am the jailor; you must show me respect!"

I jokily apologised, trying my hardest to keep a straight face.

"I didn't mean any offence, I'm sorry."

Then to try and make it better I said, "What I meant was, you are like Gollum. In the sense that you have become trapped by what happened around you. Trapped by the events that led him to being the way he is."

Blah blah blah. I was giving a long-winded bullshit

explanation and the confusion on his face grew. So I threw in a, "if you don't understand what I mean, then you're more stupid than you look."

He flipped again.

"What? What you say? I am stupid? I look stupid?"

"No, no. I don't say such a thing, you misheard me. I said you are not stupid in your look."

"You think my English is not good. You think I don't understand. You go stand over there with your arms up. You insult me; I will make things very bad for you."

I did as he said and stood up. He sat there fuming for a while and then he started laughing.

"So I am stupid? I am sitting comfortable. Tell me, your arms, they hurting yet?"

"No, I am getting used to it."

"Good, you can stay there long time."

He sat and stared. I asked to go the toilet.

"Ok, I will call somebody."

He sat there twitching around in his seat for a while. I feigned that I needed the toilet badly by putting my weigh noticeably on one leg and then the other, doing the little dance that kids do all over the world. He smiled at my apparent discomfort. After a few minutes, he got up and left the room. I put my arms down and smiled. Another small victory.

Since the first day of coming into this new block, I had been thinking it might be possible for me to make a break for it somehow. Every time I was taken to the toilet blindfolded, I would count how many steps it was to the sliding door, because every time we went past it, it would open and I would feel the hot blast from the outside world. It was something I had in the back of my head and if there was a way to use it, then I would find that way.

Once back in my room, I again checked the air conditioning pipes. This was another option I was thinking of and I still wondered if they could support my weight. I worked out how many ceiling tiles equated to my steps, I also allowed for turns. I was determined that if things got worse for me, then I must have some kind of escape plan. I started checking the computer equipment out again, I was certain there was some way of making it work, but still I couldn't get a screen working. The big chair behind the desk had a star-shaped base. One of the legs was a bit loose, so I pulled it back and forwards and after working it a while it came away. I heard a noise, so I quickly screwed it back in position with just one screw and shot back round to my side of the desk. Gollum was back, this time he was carrying a couple of sheets of A4 paper. On them were the same phone numbers as earlier. He read them out and asked if I knew them. If I said yes, he ticked them. If I said no, he looked up at me, as if to say, 'are you sure about that?'

When he was finished with the numbers, he asked about Naj and what did I know of his contacts. We had been meeting people on a daily basis; sometimes two or three meetings in a day. Naj had built up a very successful property company having worked very hard to make good contacts with all the main builders and developers. We had met so many people in such a short time that it was impossible for me to recall everyone's name.

I didn't want to say anything about the people I could remember, as it would seem like I was trying to frame anybody and everybody else and divert attention off me. I knew how these bastards' minds worked and to bring anybody else's name into the frame would be pointless. I had already told them about Mustafa and Karim - two of the dodgiest men I'd met in Dubai - and they had completely glossed over my statement. I sat for a while, then got restless waiting for Gollum to decide on his next question. He said nothing as I started to walk around the room. He scribbled something then told me he was leaving and would be back shortly. I stood rooted to the spot until the door was locked.

Continuing with my walk my head down I noticed an ant by the wall, a single ant. It wasn't moving and even as I stood over it, it remained motionless. I continued to pace around the room and every now and then I would come back to the ant, to see if there was any change. As I stood over the ant once more, I heard a knocking coming from the other side of the wall.

Dah dah dah dah dah dah dah dahd dah dah.

I sat down on the floor, with my ear to the wall and listened to the tapping. There it was again! Shit; somebody's trying to communicate! It must be Morse Code. So I started trying to work out how many dots and dashes. Dammit! Why don't I know Morse Code. If I can just remember the sequence, maybe it's obvious. Then the thought occurred to me; maybe it was the guards playing games with me to see if I would respond and try to communicate back. I didn't know what to do. Should I risk communicating? Maybe they were watching somewhere and laughing at my dilemma. I carried on walking around the room and decided to think it through. The ant had disappeared from its spot and I found it further along the wall, working its way around the periphery of the room, searching for a way out.

In my fascination with my ant friend, I hadn't even noticed the hours had passed by. My eyes were itchy and sore, although I was past the stage of being tired. I had kept the foil lids from the water containers, fashioned these into eye covers and sat back in my chair with the foil placed over my eyes like makeshift sunglasses. I just wanted to block the light out for a few hours and give my eyes a rest. I have no idea how many hours I had been awake during my detainment, I know I had maybe had a couple of hours of sleep in total. The foil covers worked amazingly well, so I propped my legs up on the desk and tried to sleep. My mind still wouldn't shut down properly and was ticking away with questions. What was the tapping all about? Was it Faz? Or Z? Maybe Raf? Does anybody on the outside know where I am? Do my family know I am still alive?

I drew an imaginary floor plan in my head. I knew that if I was going to get out of here on my own, then I had to make a break soon. The meal box was still in the room, so I opened it and looked at the contents. The plastic spoon caught my eye. I took it out of the box and broke off the spoon bit, so I was left with just the handle. I found a section of wall over in the corner and out of view of both the door and the desk. I scraped the handle until I made a sharp point. Ok, it was only plastic. But it was thick, fairly strong plastic and I figured I could do some damage with it if I had to. And anyway, a crap weapon is better than no weapon at all. I knew that during the night, after the evening meal, the place was at its quietest. This would be the best time to break free. Next, I took the wooden leg from the chair and placed it beside the door. If the cameras were watching me, the guards would have said something by now, unless they thought I was totally crazy; pacing around, salsa dancing and shadow-boxing, tampering with the ceiling tiles and talking to an insect. Right... I would stand behind the door in my usual spot.

When the door opened, whoever opened it would normally pop their head in first to see where I was, before asking my name or telling me to stand up, or put my arms up, or whatever. So if I stood behind the door, as they popped their head in, I would strike and knock them out. I would drag them inside, tie their hands with electric wires from the desk, then stick my plastic handle straight into the jugular and walk out using them as a shield. Once I was through the sliding doors, I would make a run for it and flag down a car. Then where would I go? To the British Embassy? To the apartment? I didn't have a clue where I was, I could be in the middle of nowhere. If I was lucky, maybe I could flag a taxi down. I didn't have any money, but that wouldn't matter until we'd reached the Embassy, or whatever. The biggest problem, as far as I could see, was the fact that I was in these oversized pyjamas. Nobody in their right mind would stop a car for a madman running around in his pyjamas in the middle of the night would they? It would be on the news by the morning. I would be painted as a dangerous terrorist and would probably be shot on sight if I ran into any Police. I thought about it, I tried to picture the eventualities in my mind, all the different permutations regarding an escape attempt. I got up and paced the room and caught up with my friend the ant, who was still doing the circuit. I asked him how he was and then we both carried on walking. Ants are not usually solitary creatures; they have their colonies and live happily amongst thousands of their relatives. I thought that maybe he was still here to keep me company. My new best friend. I walked round and round and round, going over everything that could happen if I made it outside.

****

Raf

A man came into the room and introduced himself as the manager. He told me he wanted me to help him, so I said I would try and do my best.

He smiled at my willingness to cooperate and pulled a sheet of paper from his pocket, which I could see was a list of some sort. He proceeded to read out telephone numbers, asking me after each one who was the person I would speak to if I called that number. I replied completely honestly, that my memory was kind of hazy and I wasn't good with remembering phone numbers at the best of times. I suggested he let me look at the list and at my phone, but he just stared at me with a look I can only say was complete hatred. He then asked me the same questions as before and threatened me with death if I kept attempting to evade answering truthfully.

****

Z

Officers would come and go throughout the day. Sometimes they were in pairs, sometimes individually. I couldn't work out a discernible pattern and I doubt that there was one. I did notice that around every eight hours there was a shift change and new faces would appear.

I was told by all of them that the British government had ordered the Dubai National Security service to detain us and extract information. I was not allowed any sleep and constantly ordered to get into different stressful and uncomfortable positions.

Chapter 8
Hold my Hand Brother

<u>Tuesday 26th July</u>

It was a little after breakfast. I was thinking that it was about time for a morning visit, when the door opened and Perky came in.

"Salaam. How are you Alam?"

There was obvious tension in his voice. I thought that after the conversation from the day before, he might have eased up a little. I was wrong; instead, he went the other way. I could see in his eyes, there was nothing but anger and hatred.

"Tired? You are tired? Would you like to sleep?"

"Yes."

"Then help yourself. We know you are holding information from us. You think this is games we play? It is very serious. You must think. Time is running out for you, Alam. You must decide if you want to see your family again. Or do you want me to be your family? There was a taxi that took the guys to London. Who was the driver?"

"I don't know any taxi."

I thought for a moment, remembering the news and whatever else I had read about the incident. I was sure the guys went to London by train.

"What are you thinking? You are trying to protect someone? You will die to protect them?"

"I am not protecting anybody."

"Then what?"

"The guys went to London by train."

"What? How do you know this?"

"It was on the news. I remember seeing it."

"Are you sure?"

"Yes, I saw it on the news."

"I don't have this information. Have you ever met the guy from Leeds?"

"No."

"You liar! You have met him. Tell me where?"

"Look I only know that he worked at a fast food place. Maybe I bought food from there. I'm tired mentally and physically drained, even doubting my own mind. But I didn't know him to speak to and I didn't know his name until it was on the news."

"So...you know him?"

"No, I do not know him."

"Why do you lie? Always you lie. You think we don't know, but we know everything."

I couldn't help laughing at the stupidity of Perky's statement.

"What is so funny? I don't think this is a joke, Alam."

"I am laughing at the irony of what you just said."

"What is irony?"

"Well you are so sure you know everything. So sure that your stupid machine knows everything."

"This is true."

"Then why don't you know I'm innocent!" I said laughing.

Perky ignored me.

"You spoke to Sharon, she told you he is from khans. What is khans?"

"That is the name of the shop where he worked."

"What did you tell Z when you saw his face on the news? In the hotel room what did you say?"

"I don't remember."

"Think. Try to remember."

"I think I said that maybe I know him."

"No, that is not what you said. You must remember. Z told us what u said."

I thought back. The only thing I remembered saying for certain was that maybe I had met him at the chip shop, if it was the one I regularly visited with my son. If he worked there, which I didn't know for sure, then he may have served me. Nothing more.

"I want to know. Why did they blow up the London?"

"I don't know."

"You do know; tell me."

"I don't know."

"But... you gave the orders."

"What orders? You're lying." I raised my voice.

"Do not raise your voice to me. I will leave. When I come back, I want to know what you said to Z when you were in the hotel room."

This shit was going round in circles again. Any thought that I might have made a small breakthrough soon gets shot down in flames. I was tired physically and mentally from the same old crap day in day out, hour after hour. The door opened a while later, but thankfully it wasn't Perky again, or worse; that horrible bastard Moonface. The guard walked in and placed a box on the table. No words were spoken. I opened the box and took out a couple of slices of bread and a slice of processed cheese. I made a small sandwich and wolfed it down.

I went over to the far wall and found my ant friend. I dropped some bread crumbs by him, not wanting him to go hungry. I thanked him for being there and asked him if he would like to stay for lunch, as I thought there might be some salad for him. I sat and watched him. For the first time my mind was completely blank. I guessed that I had reached a level of exhaustion where my brain had stopped ticking over subconsciously. The bastards were slowly chipping away at me and they were winning. I said a prayer to Allah, asking him to keep my loved ones safe.

With barely enough time to finish my lunch, Perky returned and started again, with the same questions about the chip shop guy.

"Ok, tell me what you said to Z."

"I said to him that maybe I had been served by the guy once or twice. I had bought food from that place a few times and it was perfectly possible that he had been there. It doesn't make you a criminal because you have fleeting contact with a criminal."

"No. You said that you know this guy? That is what you said to Z, that you know him, yes?"

"Look, I can't remember exactly what I said. I didn't think it was too important."

"Ok, did you go to internet city?"

"No, I don't know where it is."

"By the marina. Have you been there?"

"To the marina?"

"Yes, to the marina."

"Yes, I went there to have a meal."

"But you have not been to internet city."

"No."

"Do you know anybody who is working there?"

"No."

"Are you sure?"

"Yes, I am sure."

"Does Z have a friend who is there?"

"I don't know. You have to ask him."

"Do you know the people he does business with?"

"No."

"Do you think there is something suspicious about him?"

"Who? Z! No, definitely not."

"Does he support any groups?"

"No, I am sure of that. I have never seen Z do anything suspicious. Not ever. I have spent a lot of time with him I am sure if he had any extreme views I would have noticed them."

"Ok, enough for now. Now go stand over there. Arms in the air. Don't move."

Perky left again. I waited until no more footsteps could be heard, then I sat on the floor. I still had some pain with the blisters and itching from a couple of days earlier, but my eyes bothered me the most. It had actually become painful when I closed my eyes. I still had my makeshift protectors in my pocket, so I pulled them out and placed them over my eyes to block out the intense light. After resting a while, I checked on my little friend. He was still there doing his thing, walking the room. The usual checks were done over the next couple of hours; the only thing I asked for every now and again would be water. Sometimes they would bring me a cup if they felt generous and sometimes they just smiled and then chose to ignore me.

When lunch came, it was boiled rice and some kind of

bone with the tiniest amount of meat on it. There were three dates wrapped in foil, some lukewarm dishwater soup and a disgusting looking salad which consisted of a couple of warm lettuce leaves swimming in something yellow. I gnawed at the bone like a hungry dog and took a couple of spoons of rice. I sipped a little soup and then I tore up the lettuce and dropped it in front of my little friend. I had eaten just enough to keep me going, so I decided to pocket the dates for later. I washed my meagre rations down with the carton of water and sat back down with my foil glasses on. I heard more footsteps coming. I should have known that they wouldn't leave me in peace for long. I hid my foil glasses and stood to attention. My buddy Gollum entered.

"Salaam."

"Salaam."

"You drink plenty of water; there is a big pile of bottles and cups in the back room. They are all yours."

"Yes, I'm trying to keep hydrated."

"Why? Is room too hot for you?" He laughed. I didn't think it was too funny.

"No, it's fine."

I didn't dare say, but every time somebody came in they would adjust it to their own liking, then turn it up when they left, so the temperature fluctuated constantly through the day. In general it was way too hot during the day and icy cold in the night. To complain was just asking for the fluctuations to become ever more extreme.

I asked to go the toilet and Gollum went off and arranged a guard. The guard turned up, blindfolded and cuffed me and led me away. We walked the forty five steps. Swoosh. The glass doors opened and the hot air rushed in.

This guard came into the toilets with me. He took off the blindfold and told me to be quick. He stayed inside with me, so there was no chance for me to try the window again. Never mind, this could be the guard who gets a chair leg around the head. That'll teach him. I did my thing and then the guard took me back to my room. I enjoyed my little walks to the toilet and back, particularly when the sliding doors opened and I could feel the heat outside. Sometimes I would hear voices chattering away. It made me think there was something more out there than just the four walls that I saw most of the day. We got back to my cell; the guard issued the standard instructions. Stand there. Put your arms up. Don't move. I waited till the footsteps faded, then I put my arms down and looked for my friend. Before I could find him, I heard the door go, so I quickly got back in place. Gollum came back in with another list in his hand.

"Alam I will read out numbers for you. You tell me if you recognise them."

He started to read out the numbers, stuttering and stumbling at times, so I would repeat them back to him and confuse him even more. We went back and forwards for a while and then it hit me. I had a fucking brilliant idea.

"Look, I can't remember numbers like this. I am tired and can't think straight. I don't memorise numbers, I store them in my phone and when I want to call somebody I input their name and get it from the phonebook. I never pay attention to what the number is. Do you know all the numbers for everybody in your phone?"

He shook his head.

"So…if you can bring my phone, I will look up the numbers in the directory and I can give you real answers.

Don't you think this is a good idea? It will help both of us, don't you agree?"

I nodded my head to encourage him that I was right. I figured if I could just get my hands on my phone, maybe I could make a call. No, that would be impossible. I could press a few buttons, pretend it's a new phone and I'm still learning the shortcuts and while I'm playing dumb I could send a text message. He sat and I could see his brain slowly digesting what I said.

"Ok….yes it may help. I will come back."

I sat there and waited for Gollum's return. I felt excited at the prospect of sending out a covert message. And if I was caught? Well, it would be worth a beating, as long as I was successful. I waited and waited. What was taking so long? I bet he was just fucking with me. I grew impatient and paced around the room. It was a pretty easy task for Gollum; bring the fucking phone to me and I'll tell you who I called and what their numbers were. Come on, come on. How long should he be taking? Gollum finally returned.

"Alam it is not possible. Your phone is locked away. Maybe tomorrow I can get it, but for now you must try to remember without it."

I tried not to look too disappointed, but I felt upset. I really believed I would get a message to the outside world and I'd built myself up to take the inevitable beating that would follow. So we went through more names and numbers. Some I recognised, some I didn't. I played along, using the same line about the phonebook and my terrible memory and insisting I would give better answers tomorrow, when my phone was in my possession. He fucked off eventually, so I took out my foil shades and placed them over my eyes. They were so uncomfortable;

scratching my skin as I had to press them down to make them stay in place. But they served a purpose, keeping the glare out and allowing me some semblance of rest. I must have semi-dozed off, as I awoke with a start as a key turned in the lock. I didn't hear any footsteps approaching, so it was lucky that I just about had time to slide the shades into my pocket and stand up straight.

Oh, it was just the evening meal. I use the word meal in the loosest sense of the word. Some slop, I think it was supposed to be a curry. I had a small spoonful, but it tasted foul. I ate the soggy salad and drank all the soup for the first time. I waited a while for the so-called meal to digest, then went through my routine of press-ups sit ups, shadow boxing and salsa. I noticed my body was struggling with the routine and had weakened with each day. I persevered until I felt exhausted, then I sat and rested. Daffy came by later in the evening. He was trying extra hard to be nice, but his falseness was all too apparent. He asked if I liked Arabic food and when I said it was Ok, but a little bland for my liking, he looked visibly offended.

"You went to Karama. You went with Z and Rafique?"

"Yes."

"You eat at the Ravi's restaurant."

"Yes."

"It is Pakistani food. It is not good!" He pulled a face and spat on the floor. "You like the Pakistani food?"

"Yeah, it's Ok.....better than Arabic food."

If looks could kill. He glared at me for a second, then he turned round and swung the monitor around to face him. Admiring himself, he must have remembered he was trying to be nice.

"Tell me, so I can help you."

One eye on me and one on the monitor.

"You are my brother, Alam. Hum tumara haat pakar gey tum go door lay jay inga. I will hold your hand and take you far away."

"I don't want to go anywhere with you. I only want to go back to England."

"Why? It is dangerous; they will kill you. Vo tum say goli mare do gay. They will shoot you."

"I don't care. I will take my chances."

"You are safe here," Daffy said with a stupid grin. How the fuck did he figure that out, the stupid bastard.

"I don't care. I want to be unsafe in England."

"Deko deko tum humara bhay hay, Alam. You are my brother."

I wanted to say to him 'Oh please, spare me your bullshit!' I was tiring of this charade, it was insulting my intelligence. As he carried on with this nonsense, I zoned out. I could see his mouth moving, but couldn't hear the words. In my head I pictured myself coshing him over the head with the chair leg and putting my blade in his neck. I bet the fucker would cry like a baby. He got tired of playing at being mister nice guy and left me alone. Thank god for that. I waited for silence, then set about examining the room again. This time, I started fiddling with one of the cabinets, to see if I could get to the camera. I managed to squeeze two fingers through the gap and the glass shelf above it slid about an inch. I was applying downward pressure on it to make it move, as it was impossible to get a grip on it. The back of it fell down into the gap and got jammed. Oh shit. I tried my hardest to adjust it back, but the bloody thing was well and truly stuck. I couldn't straighten it or put it back to normal, so I gave up and prayed that nobody would notice.

The checks were on-going, although I suspected the time gaps were larger between them, I had no real way of telling if this was true. I was able to close my eyes and rest them, but still a proper sleep was elusive, as any sound would make me jump up in anticipation of the door opening. Between interrogations I looked for my friend. I walked the perimeters of the wall but on this occasion I couldn't find him so I went round again, extra slowly but still no sign. I felt tears trickle down my face….he'd left me. All the time he was there my spirits were lifted. Now he was gone all hope was lost. I sat down and closed my eyes and it was as if a huge vault of memories was suddenly opened. Happy childhood memories flooded back; so vivid, so real that every now and again I would open my eyes and remind myself where I was. Thoughts and memories that I had been suppressing had come to me in my state of weakness. I revelled in the happy thoughts and then I told myself that I could not allow myself to wallow any longer. The vault closed and I would not be opening it again.

My friend mister Booty Wax turned up that day. He told me he normally only works in the other building, but somehow was sent over here for a change. I was glad to see him. No questions, just a normal conversation - how are you, are you Ok, do you need anything - that kind of thing. I told him that all I ever really needed was more water, so he left for a couple of minutes, returning with four containers. With that, he told me that he had to go before someone started asking his whereabouts, but he would return later if he could.

****

Raf

I had been standing for hours. The guards would just watch me, saying nothing. Sometimes they told me to stand on one leg and then hours later they would tell me change to the other leg. Physically, I felt exhausted. Mentally, I was so drained with the constant questioning and the same questions time after time. I was still sweating profusely and despite promising to get my medication, it still hadn't materialised. The constant death threats and promise of lifetime imprisonment were also not helping with my mental state, so I had difficulty answering their questions about what calls I had made during my stay in Dubai. They seemed particularly interested in why I had been ringing Faz sometimes four or five times a day and didn't seemed convinced with my honest explanation that I was not familiar with the roads, so I would ring him if I was lost.

A list of phone numbers was placed in front of me. Some were from England, some from Dubai. I recognised maybe half of them but the others I could not really place without checking my mobile. I told the interrogator this and he went off to get my phone. When he returned I scrolled through the numbers and gave him names and reasons why I had spoken to them. He was also curious about how I knew them, scribbling down all my replies as we went through the list.

I didn't know if anyone in the outside world knew what was happening to me and my friends and if they were taking any action to help us. While I was going through the numbers with my interrogator, I managed to send a text message to three of my friends in the UK. The text said –

we are in prison in Dubai they blame us for London bombing don't reply to this get help

The guy was too busy to have noticed, so I carried on giving him more numbers and names. Eventually he had filled his sheet with enough information, so he took my phone off me and left the room. I prayed that the message would get through and that somebody would try to help me. A guard came in and I was told to stand up. He marked out a circle in the thick pile carpet around me with his foot and told me not to move out of the circle or I would be severely punished.

I settled in my spot. I was happy that I had got the message out; I had faith that someone would inform the authorities about us and our ordeal would be over soon. There was the sound of feet rushing to my door. Click click, the door flew open. The guard rushed at me and slapped me hard across my face, first one side and then the other. I realised he had my phone in his hand.

"Mr Siddique you are in very much trouble. You sent a message to your friend."

He shoved the phone into my face; my eyes struggled to focus. The stupid bastards had replied back to the message.

"If this is Raf give me name of ur son if Z give me name of ur dog."

He pulled the phone away.

"You are very stupid. So stupid. Now you will suffer. Do not move."

He eyed me with pure disgust his nostrils flaring and teeth baring, I thought he was going to hit me again. But he just left the room and I stood there shaking. I could not believe it. I thought to myself this is it. They're going to beat the shit out of me now and kill me for sure. The small consolation was that the message had got through. Even though I couldn't reply to the message that had been spotted, then at least they and the two other recipients would maybe start asking around about me. It wasn't much, but it cheered me up a little.

****

Z

I had the same routine every day. Days blurred together as I endured round the clock questioning. Same questions, same answers. The only respite I got was the prayer times when they would allow me to go the bathroom, get washed and come back in the room and pray. Sometimes, to get myself some extra rest, I would stay in the lying position on the floor. If they came into the room they would leave and come back later when they thought I would have finished. It may have been wrong to use such a time to my advantage, but in that situation, I really didn't care.

Chapter 9
Important Information

<u>Wednesday 27th July 2005</u>

I smelled the ood on him before he came into the room. Once you smell the Arabian perfume, you never forget it. It seems like everyone in Dubai had a penchant for the sickly scent that is made from amber. Some used it sparingly, others far more freely. One of those with a love for splashing it all over was my friend, Gollum. I commented that it was very nice that he was wearing ood.

"What? How you know this? You rude to me again?"

"No, no. I bought some a few days ago. I like it very much. I wish I had some, I smell so bad."

"What, you have not showered?"

"No, not for many days now."

"Ok, I will arrange it."

A guard came in, blindfolded and cuffed me and then led me down the corridor. Forty five steps later, I heard the 'swoosh' as the door opened. I was outside. The warm air engulfed my body and the scent of flowers filled my nose. I took a deep breath and imagined what it looked like. My head was pushed down as I was bundled into the back of a car.

The car was driven off at high speed. I anticipated the

turns and the huge arc and I smiled to myself when they happened. We did the usual slide to a halt. I was pulled out, banging my head in the process and dragged into the other building. I stood in front of one gate as it was opened by a guard. I was pushed through and told to wait while it was locked behind me. Another gate opened in front of me, I was pushed through and followed the same routine as it closed behind me. My arms were then grabbed on either side and as I was walked forwards the guy on my left said something in Arabic. Then in broken English he said,

"You are strong."

He started rubbing his hand on my thigh, then on the front of my thigh, creeping up towards my groin. The dirty bastard was trying to touch me up! Remarkably, I didn't freeze up. I just got angry, very angry. I pictured the two guys holding me; first the pervert. I figured I could elbow him straight in the throat and then deal with the one on my right. I could throw my hands over his head and choke the life out of him. But it crossed my mind that as I was already behind lock and key it could just make things worse for me if I attack my guards. Was it best to just let things happen? It's easy to say in all bravado that I would do this and I would do that; for men it's a macho thing and being raped is probably the most humiliating thing possible for the ego. Unless you are faced with it in reality, you don't know how you would react.

I made up my mind. I was going to kill these fuckers, or at least try my best to, before they got any further. Then supposing that they don't kill me, maybe they'll just beat me senseless and then rape me every day for the rest of my life. Hmm. Lose, lose situation. What the fuck do I do? I stumbled into the shower block, the cuffs were taken off and the blindfold removed. I looked up and could see the CCTV camera watching me. I had a good look at the dirty bastard's face, the one who had been touching me. He had a Hitler 'tache and an evil looking face. There was no humanity in this one for sure. He had close set eyes that made him look inbred. Talk about stereotyping; this bastard definitely looked like a pervert.

"Be quick. Three minutes. Hurry up."

He stood and watched me undress, unable to take his eyes off me. He reached up with his stick and adjusted the camera to point away from us.

I prepared myself for the worst. I undressed quickly and got into the shower. The water slowly dribbled out, boiling hot, but with no power. I soaped up and shampooed my hair but I didn't close my eyes in case the guard approached me. I kept my eyes on him constantly and he stood his ground. The scabs from the previous treatment were peeling off and some got knocked off as I soaped myself. I quickly rinsed off the best I could.

A dish dash was handed to me. A horrible stripy thing that looked like it had been made out of old bed linen. Dirty, piss-stained bed linen. never once took his eyes off me. He cuffed me first, then blindfolded me and dragged me off down the corridor. I was walking at a steady pace but this bastard was literally dragging me along. He pushed me intentionally into the wall, then into the gate. When we were back outside, walking to the car, he tripped me up and as I stumbled he kicked the back of my leg. And then to top it all off, he bashed my head against the car as he pushed me in the back. We roared off back to the other building and I was bounced off the walls all the way back to my room. I'm not entirely sure, but I had a real suspicion that didn't like me. Before too long, Gollum was back to see me.

"You smell better. You look better. Ok, Alam. You can sit down. Talk to me."

"What do you want to know?"

"Talk to me. Tell me anything."

So I started to question him on his life in general and his work. I asked open questions that made him talk. People like to talk, especially about themselves. I asked - Do you enjoy your work? What made you get into this? Is there anything different you would like to do? Where do want to visit? Where have you visited? What hobbies or pastimes do you enjoy?

He told me that his father had pulled some strings and got him the job. I made a big effort to increase the rapport with him; I had to make him believe in me if my next plan was to work. Yesterday I had allowed myself to feel down after losing my friend the ant, but I had not given up yet. Not while there was any fight left in me. We talked at length, I did my best to flatter him and butter him up.

"You're an intelligent guy. You have been here for many years; it's about time they promoted you. Would you change things if they made you the boss? What would you change?"

Then I dropped it on him.

"Look, I have some very important information."

He sat upright.

"It is very, very important." I emphasised the second very.

"You can tell me, Alam."

"I trust you and only you. I want to help you by giving this information to you. But..." I paused for effect, to see if he was taking the bait. He leaned forward in his chair.

"You have to help me too. It is very important. I need you to speak to the British Embassy. You must get them to come here."

"That is not possible! I cannot ask them to come here."

"Ok, why don't you ring them? You will be next to me, you can write down what I am saying."

"Huaah, you just want to speak to them so you can tell them you are here."

"But you told me already; they know I am here, they give the order for us to be picked up, yes?"

"Err... yes."

"Look. I will not say my name, I promise you. This information has to be given directly to them; there are a lot of people in danger."

"Give me the information, I will pass it on."

"No that is not possible. You will pass it your boss, then he will pass it to his boss and things will become confused. By the time the Embassy starts acting on it, it will be too late and people will die. Do you want that to happen? Do you want people to die?"

"No, of course not."

"Ok, this information is very specific. You can be a hero; they will have to promote you. You will be like James Bond. You know who James Bond is?"

"Yes, of course."

"James Bond is a hero. You want to be the hero? Think about it. After all these days I have been here, you are the one who got the information out of me. It was you. How proud will your father and your mother be when you get promotion because you got information?"

"I don't have the number for the Embassy."

"You have a phone book, or why don't you call directory inquiries?"

"My phone signal is not so good."

"Are you afraid? I have noticed how the others don't treat you with enough respect. Is that right?"

I was nodding my head, prompting him to follow.

"They think you don't know how to do job. They think you will never be better than them. It is easy to see what they think. I can see it on their faces and so can you."

Another nod.

"You want to be somebody? Then this is your chance to show them isn't it?"

More nodding.

"Maybe you are scared your boss will think you did something without his permission. But you are brave and very clever. You got the information from me, you have used initiative and you will have saved lives. After all these years they will promote you; maybe you will be your boss's boss then…." I started to raise my voice and pointing my finger at him I said at the top of my voice, "YOU WILL BE A HERO!"

He looked at me and gulped. He swallowed hard and I could see his mouth was dry. His eyes were in the middle distance; his brain was ticking so fast, his breathing was shallow and high. He was definitely weighing up everything I had said. In my head I was willing him to take the bait. Come on. Come on, Gollum. Do it. Do it. Come on. DO IT!

"I will go and get the number," he finally said and off he rushed.

As he locked the door behind himself, I started pacing the room impatiently. This could be it. This could be the beginning of the end of this nightmare. I hope the idiot falls for it. Of course I'm going to tell the Embassy who I am! You better fucking believe it. He had confirmed to me what I had known deep down all along, which was that the Embassy was not aware that me and my friends were being held here, or anywhere else.

I have no idea how long it was before he returned, gingerly opening the door he came in, followed close behind by Fatty. That wanker Gollum didn't have the bollocks to look me in the eye. Instead Fatty came in all puffed up like a fucking pigeon, doing a mating dance, all smug and proud.

"So..Mr Alam.. you have information....but you have demands?"

"I have no demands.....the information I have is very special and it needs to be handled in a sensitive manner."

In for a penny, in for a pound. I've come this far with this ploy; I may as well keep it going to its conclusion.

"Mr Alam, I have all the consulate staff on my telephone. I can call anybody and they will come here."

"Ok then, call somebody...and make sure they bring some I.D with them."

If this fucker thought I was going to fall for any traps, he better think again. I was one step ahead. I was in control of this game, or so I thought.

"But first, before I call them, I have to know that the information you have is valuable."

"Listen to me, the information I have is valuable. You don't need to make that decision. All you want is recognition...you are going to say you have information from a source and try to claim credit for it. You cannot explain this to them, it has to be presented in the way that I will explain to them."

"Mr Alam, you have to tell me."

"No ...I don't," I said defiantly. This fat fucker was being awkward.

"Many people will die because you don't want me to communicate with the consulate directly. Just ring them. You hold the phone and I will speak to them."

"No, I cannot do that until I know what it is. I cannot waste the time of important men."

"You are wasting valuable time right now. Maybe you do not care if the people die."

He didn't say a word. He smiled his false smile, the frustration apparent in his eyes. I smiled back, but my smile was more a mocking gesture than anything friendly.

"Mr Alam, if you cooperate it will be better for you."

"I am cooperating, but you are not accepting my cooperation."

"Tell me something; you Pakistanis are terrorists. You want to blow people up in the name of Islam, but you people know nothing about Islam. You are not Muslims."

"No, you are wrong. The majority of terrorists are Arabs." I emphasised the word Arab. "You Arabs come over to India and Pakistan to teach religion, building religious schools, picking sympathetic teachers who can manipulate young minds into your way of thinking. You people teach them to be terrorists so you can carry on and enjoy the comfortable life you have here by taking attention away from yourselves. 9/11 was carried out by Arabs, wasn't it? Or have you forgotten? There were no Pakistani's or Indians involved. 11 out of the 16 hijackers had received money from Dubai, so don't stand there and tell me that Pakistanis are terrorists, when you and your country are terrorists. You are the ones who support the Taliban and look at the mess they cause. You are hypocrites."

I was so angry, I couldn't stop myself, "so fuck you and your fucking country, I've had enough of your shit already. Get the fucking Embassy on the phone now!"

He rushed over and hit me; two slaps across the face with the back of his hand.

"Who do you think you are talking to, you bastard!"

It was the first time anybody had sworn at me since my incarceration. Gollum stood over by the desk, open-mouthed like he was frozen in shock. The frustration had boiled over in Fatty and I could tell that he wanted to do more damage to me. Gollum snapped out of his stupor and said something in Arabic. Fatty pulled back from me, obviously struggling to restrain himself. His face burning red. Excellent I was beginning to get under the skin of these knob heads. My fist clenched tight another little victory.

"Ok, I will leave you now. If you want to talk to me, ask for me. I will come back again."

He said something to Gollum, then he left the room. Gollum looked over at me and then averted his eyes.

"I thought we had a deal. I trusted you. I wanted to help you."

"But...but he is my boss."

"He will always be your boss. You will never be a boss; you don't have the courage or initiative to do something by yourself. You are an order taker, not an order giver. And you are a coward."

He looked totally demoralised. The way I spoke to him was still part of my plan to get him on the defensive. I wasn't sure if I was going to be able to use Gollum in the way I had hoped, but I still needed to gain the upper hand over him, if only for my own satisfaction.

There was silence. Gollum looked like a naughty schoolboy who had just been told off. Maybe there was still a chance to manipulate him. I was fuming, but I was trying not to show it. ...Fuck fuck fuck fuck. If this bastard had just let me make that call... Ok, back to the drawing board. I had to think of something else. Only one thing I can do; give them what little I had.

"Go get your boss. I can't have it on my conscience that people will die. I care... I just hope your boss does not make a mess of this."

He scurried off and returned quickly with Fatty, who strutted in arrogantly.

"So, Alam. You are ready to talk? So tell me."

"First I want to make it clear, I tell you this because I want to help. Not because you frighten or scare me, but because I care."

"Yes, go on."

"Some months ago my son's mother Anna told me that she was at a phone shop that is in Beeston, near Leeds."

"Yes." Fatty said as he leaned in towards me. Trying his best not to breathe too hard

"She was there to buy a new phone and the guy who runs the shop was in the back room talking to somebody and when he turned round, she saw it was a guy called Raza. She knows him because he was her friend Kelly's boyfriend and had been to Anna's house a few times. She didn't like him because he was always talking about war and violence and how things should change. He would say things like he was sick of this person, or sick of this government, we need people to sit up and take notice etc. There is only one way; we have to bring jihad here and open the people's eyes."

"Go on..." Fatty was really interested now. Gollum was scribbling away furiously.

"Anna was frightened, so she left the shop. When she went to the newsagent, the owner was talking about the local mosque with one of the other customers. The guy was saying that there were too many foreigners there now. Too many Somali's, Iraqis and Kurds and all they did was turn every debate to jihad. The shop owner sympathised and told the customer that he had noticed the same thing and so he had started to go to the other mosque."

"Yes, this is all very interesting," Fatty interrupted. "But what has this to do with the Embassy?"

"When she came out the shop, there were a load of kids handing out leaflets advertising a talk for that Friday night. The guy from the phone shop walked over to her and said that he had seen her leave his shop and he knew she had been listening to his conversation. Anna said she didn't know what he was talking about, but he pulled her close to him and whispered in her ear that he knows where she lives and he hoped she will not make trouble by repeating anything she'd heard, or there would be problems for her and her family. She was scared. She told me what happened; obviously I want to know, because my son has been threatened in a roundabout way. From what she said and because of what the newspapers said about where the plot originated, then I think these guys are behind what has happened. I need to speak to the Embassy, so they can guarantee Anna and my son's safety and then she can point out all the people involved."

Gollum was still frantically scribbling down everything I was saying.

"Anything else?"

"No."

The bullshit was flowing freely off the top of my head. Maybe Fatty would pass this information on. Maybe Anna would be questioned and realise it was me who had made these claims and start asking the Embassy to find my whereabouts. So many maybes and I just needed one definite.

Fatty almost ran out of the room. He paused at the door and asked if I was hungry. I shook my head and off he went with his good news.

"I hope your boss is very careful," I said to Gollum. "I don't want anything to happen to my son." My voice slow and deliberate for extra emphasis.

****

Z

I was on the floor, prostrate in the praying position so that whenever the guards came to check on me, they would not say anything and quickly close the door. This gave me breathing space and time to rest. Obviously I could only do this at prayer times and the rest of the time I was told to stand with my arms raised, either to the side or straight up in the air. I was in my position when the fat guard suddenly burst in, looking very pleased about something. The cynic in me sensed that it wasn't going to be good news. He motioned for me to come over and sit down. Excitedly he said,

"Mr Alam has given us good information. It is very good information. Now it is your turn. You must give us information. Tell me what do you know."

I sat there thinking about what he'd said. What could Alam have said? There was nothing he could say, was there? Maybe the stress of all this had become too much, maybe they had broken him. To save himself, maybe he pointed the finger at one of us. I didn't think he would be the first one to break; I figured that would be Faz if anybody. Of course, there was the faint possibility that he had actually heard or seen something. No, I couldn't believe that. Alam was a straight down the middle kind of guy; he wouldn't know anything about any terrorists. No, they were lying to me. I cursed myself for nearly falling for their mind games. This is how they work, isn't it? They play you off against each other, tell you one is talking, that you are being blamed for everything. I wasn't going to fall for their lies.

I replied, "I do not know anything. I want to make a phone call to my wife."

"This is not possible. I want information from you. Give me something."

I shook my head, his annoyance with me all too clear. He got up and hurried out again, a guard came in and pointed to my spot in the middle of the floor, so I walked over and resumed my previous position.

****

Alam

Pinky and Perky came by later on in the day. Perky had his usual clutch of papers with him. We all sat down together; them on their side of the desk and me on mine. Perky was busily reading the papers and Pinky was just staring at me. Every time I caught his eye he would look down or look away. Perky looked up.

"Alam; why?"

"Why?" I looked at him puzzled.

"Why you always blame Anna?"

"I have not blamed Anna."

"Yes, here today you are making the allegation that she

know about dangerous people."

"It's the truth. I told your boss everything I know."

"I do not believe, I think you blame her. Why? Is because she cannot defend herself against what you say?"

"She can defend herself if your boss passes the information on in the correct manner."

"You are lying, I do not believe you."

Then he suddenly flipped and started screaming and shouting at me.

"You are a liar! This is not true what you have said."

His face went bright red with the exertion I sat there unfazed, not even blinking. Looking across at Pinky, even he was surprised at the outburst. When he had tired himself out, Perky left the room. Pinky sat there still making no eye contact whatsoever. He scribbled something on the scrap of paper, spoke to himself in Arabic and then shuffled out of the room. I sat there motionless, in front of the desk as nobody had told me to move. After waiting a while just to make sure the coast was clear, I pulled out my foil shades and placed them over my eyes. Kicked my legs up and listened.

The usual routine of door opening and asking my name carried on. The evening meal was brought, another dire affair. I walked, hopped and did my exercise routine but my coordination was definitely deteriorating further. I felt weak and clumsy, but reasoned that it was to be expected.

****

Z

Having endured another day of meaningless questioning, I finished my dinner, if that's the right word for it and assumed I was in for the typical evening of sporadic visits and no sleep. So it was a surprise when the guard came in with handcuffs and a blindfold. I was led outside the building and put in a car. A short while later I was back at the first building. I was dragged out and taken to the original cell from the first day. At least it had a bed, so I thought I would try and get some sleep. I lay down and closed my eyes and thought I was dreaming, because I swear I could hear my name being called. I lay there for a few moments with my eyes open. No, I must have fallen asleep straight away, it....there it was again. It was my name being called out! I lay on the floor by the letterbox where the food parcels came through and I heard my name again. It took me a moment, but I recognised the voice was Raf's and he was in the cell next door to mine. We spoke, I asked if he was Ok, he asked about me and we both wondered about the others. He mentioned that Alam and Faz were both still here, because he had seen their shoes when he was taken without a blindfold to see the Major.

The intercom in my cell crackled, so we stopped talking. The guard came and opened my cell door, looking rather disgruntled. He asked me if I had spoken with Raf and I replied yes. He told me I better come out and follow him. I was led down the corridor, took a turn to the left and then followed the passage right to the end, to the very last cell. I looked inside and wasn't impressed. There was a single blood-soaked mattress on the floor and the room stank of piss and shit. He pushed me in and locked the door. I was left in this cesspit for hours with no air-conditioning. The smell was unbearable and I had to stuff my cuff in my mouth to stop me puking.

****

Alam

It was sometime in the morning. I had sat down on the floor with my back propped against the wall. I was so tired; my mind was just running with thoughts over which I had no control. I thought about the day my father passed away. Every detail of that sad day went through my mind and at first the tears were just coming one at a time, but the more I thought of it, the more the floodgates opened. As I sat crying unashamedly, my head felt as though it was ready to explode. I knew that I was losing it, so I forced myself to stop focussing on my father's passing and instead tried to think good thoughts about his life.

My father had been born in India and was one of thirteen children. His childhood was tough, he was the eldest male. But my father was a strong man, physically as well as mentally and when the opportunity came for him to move to England in his late teens, he took the bull by the horns. He had worked incredibly hard and created a life for himself, all the while sending money back home to support his mother, brothers and sisters. His advice to me was always to work hard and to be honest. My childhood was a happy one. Dad would spoil me when he could and always told everyone how proud he was of me. I always asked him to tell me about his childhood in India, as this part of my heritage fascinated me. He told me of the violence during the partition of India and Pakistan and how his family had been left penniless by the move. One of his favourite tales was about how once he was in the woods miles away from home, foraging for food and berries, when he was spotted by a bandit. My father was petrified at the time, as he had witnessed the bandits beating people in his village. My dad just stood frozen to the spot when the man had seen him, but the bandit shared some bread with him, gave him some fruit and walked him back to the edge of the village.

We had lived in London for a while, but after my father injured his spine he decided that we would return to Yorkshire. My brothers and sisters concentrated on their schooling, while I went on to college and worked part time supporting the family. After college, I went to university for a year, but I gave up when I received the offer of a full time job as a financial adviser. I talked over the job with my father, who was happy that I would be providing more for the family. He had no education to speak of and realised that hard work and supporting the family were more important than any piece of paper.

In 1993 mum decided to go visit her sisters in Pakistan. Bored with work, I decided I needed a break, so I would accompany her. It wasn't my first choice of destination but I thought now was a good time to get some culture and see some of my heritage. We spent six weeks there, travelling all over, meeting family and friends. A few weeks after we returned, dad complained one morning that he had pains in his arms and chest and then he fell over, unable to breathe properly. At the hospital they diagnosed a cardial infarction better known as a heart attack.

A few months later, with dad well rested, my uncle suggested that we take a look at a small business that was for sale nearby. We all had a good look around, checked all the paperwork and I looked at the sales figures. With everything satisfactory, we decided to go for it. The purchase went smoothly and on the 10th of October we opened our doors for the first time. It was a small village shop, selling newspapers, convenience goods and sandwiches. It wasn't huge, but it was all ours and it meant we had a steady income for the family and plenty of staff to look after it. Dad wasn't involved too much and over the next year he took less and less of an interest. He often complained of restricted breathing and chest pains and as a lifetime smoker it was to be expected. Even after the scare earlier in the year, he hadn't given up fully, just cut back to a few a day. Dad was taken into hospital for a number of days and the family took turns to visit. I was in the shop in the early morning, sorting out the papers, when the hospital rang and said I should come to the hospital, as my father had been found dead in his sleep. I turned and punched the wall. Mum came down the stairs. She paused halfway as she realised what had happened. I rushed up and hugged her tight. I said 'mum he's gone, he's gone' and we stood there in the middle of the stairs, hugging and crying.

Chapter 10
Tomorrow You Die

The door opened, Gollum came in with my food box. He placed it on the table and looked at me sitting there. I must have cut a pathetic figure, my shoulders bowed and hunched forwards, with bloodshot red eyes from my crying.

"Alam, come, you must eat."

I leaned forward and picked up the box. I held it in my lap, but I wasn't hungry so I didn't open it.

"You have been crying, now you regret what you have done?"

"No I have not done anything. Tell me are your mother and father alive?"

"Yes, Alam."

"Let me tell you; the saddest day of my life was when I lost my father."

I explained the events leading up to it; how he had been feeling unwell, having shortness of breath. How I was with him at the time when he felt a pain in his arm. I had called the doctor and then called for an ambulance. Once up at the hospital they had started taking blood and carrying out ECG tests and then in a matter of hours it was determined that he had suffered a full blown heart attack. I was crying and they had taken him away to intensive care. I was told to go home and ring up later to see how he was. At home, my mother went into hysterics when I had told her.

Gollum was looking at me with a look that I guessed was supposed to be of sympathy. He didn't interrupt my narrative, but I noticed that he glanced at his watch in a subtle way. Not so subtle that I didn't see him. I carried on with my story.

"I remember walking into my father's room at the hospital and seeing him lying there dead. I broke down and was completely inconsolable. The nurses came in and I started shouting and swearing at them 'why why didn't you help him? How could you let him die?' My mother tried to calm me, but to no avail. I sat by his side and held his hand."

I sat there crying like a baby. Gollum didn't say a word. I told him I was not scared to die. All the threats they made to me meant nothing. Go ahead and kill me.

"Calm down, Alam. No one is going to kill you."

"I want you to know that no matter how clever you think you are, somebody will come here maybe in six months or six years, but they will come to find the truth. And when they do, my friend, this country that you think is so great and modern will be shown to be nothing more than the piece of shit that it really is."

He looked at me and spoke slowly, with no emotion in his words.

"Go stand over there. You cannot speak to me like this, who do you think you are? Tony Bush or George Blair? Nobody will come for you. You are worthless."

"That is where you are wrong! Here you only care if somebody has money. You like and respect the man because he is rich, but in England, if you are a British citizen, it does not matter if you have one million pounds or one pound because you are British citizen. You are protected and looked after. This country is nothing. And you are nothing. Your country is rubbish. You think you have freedom, with your greedy Sheiks controlling everything. Your country is full of prostitutes and drug dealers and con men. Everyone knows your ports are used to transport drugs and you turn a blind eye. People are laundering money from illegal activities around the world. You see them walking around with suitcases and even shopping bags filled with all different currencies, but nothing is done. You think you are good Muslims? Slavery was abolished years ago, but in this country you wouldn't know it, the way you treat your workers. You are nothing and your country is nothing. It is sad so many people come here and yet they don't know truth of your empty country without a soul. You don't scare me; none of your friends scare me. You are all weak people hiding behind the money. Fuck you and your fucking little tin pot country."

Gollum swivelled in his chair. His expression was one of a confused, scolded child. Maybe he didn't understand a lot of what I was blurting out, but I'm certain he got the gist of what I was inferring about his country. He got up and left without a word. Hopefully he would report what I'd said, or with luck it had been recorded, so all the guards could listen to what I thought about their poxy country. I didn't care anymore. Let them do what they want.

I had a food box delivered later; my dinner was accompanied by a fly. Usually I would shoo away the fly, but I was happy for it to crawl around on the back of my palm and over my finger. A new friend to replace my ant.

We spoke at length and I told him all about the happenings earlier in the day. My new friend listened patiently without interrupting me once.

****

The next morning

Gollum came in with my breakfast box. One drink and a couple of dates. No stale bread or processed cheese. I guess I'm on punishment rations. Gollum sat down in the big chair, staring at me, as if studying something. He swivelled slowly side to side. I stood in position maintaining eye contact...he spoke.

"Tell me something."

"What?"

"The two stripes you have in your beard, what do they mean?"

"They don't mean anything."

"No Alam, they do mean something. I have been thinking all night. I was not sleeping, it was on my mind. Suddenly I sit up in my bed and realise; aah yes ....now I know who Mr Alam is ....Two stripes in your beard, hmm two stripes. Taliban means two students, so two stripes means two students. It is your sign that you support them."

Gollum smiled, looking really pleased with himself. The fool. Time to play with him some more.

"What? How did you think of this? Nobody in my organisation has ever thought of this. Nobody knew why I had two stripes, but you... you are very clever to think this."

He looked even more pleased with himself.

"You think I am powerful and have a big organisation. What will they do when they know you have me? What will they do to Dubai?"

Gollum didn't look quite so cocky.

"Can I have drink of water?"

"Ok, I will get," he said and got up immediately to get me one. He returned quickly, accompanied by somebody I hadn't seen before. The new guy handed the water to me. I took it and looked at it then looked at them. I waited a minute or two.

"Have you no sealed cups?"

"No this is from the bottle."

They both stared. I raised the glass slowly to my lips and pretended I was about to sip it, then quickly withdrew it, half spilling it.

"Ha! You think I am stupid. Do you know how many people try to poison me and kill me? You think you are so clever that I will drink this poison?"

I poured some onto my sleeve while they both looked at me, their eyes wide in astonishment. I spat on it then rubbed it into the cloth and took a sniff.

"You think I don't know what is in this? I will not drink it."

"I...I don't know what..." the new guy stuttered.

"Truth serum. Sodium pentothal!"

It's amazing what you pick up in Hollywood movies. I placed the cup on the table and they both left the room in a panic; Gollum taking the water with him. I sat down on the floor and chuckled to myself that I must be mad. Maybe this would infuriate or excite them thinking they had caught somebody of great importance.

Gollum returned by himself, clutching a few sheets of paper in one hand and a pen in the other. He sat down and asked me to sit at the table. He placed the paper and pen in front of me.

"Ok Alam, write down everything you know. I want you to write...you understand what I want you to write...yes?"

I knew that he was after a confession. Along with his superiors he must have felt I had broken down to the point where it was now possible to get exactly what they wanted; a false confession.

"Are you ready for the truth? Do you want to know who I am?"

There was method to my madness. I figured I had one last chance and this was it; all or nothing. I began scribbling away. Gollum's phone went off, so he rushed out of the room. On the first sheet I wrote down...

I am not a guilty man

I have told the truth about the 7th July London bombings

I have done nothing wrong

I have nothing to hide in England

I have nothing to hide from the British government

I do not have a police record

I have never given money to these men or any group

I do not support the action taken

The events on 7th July are terrorist attacks on the British government

You have managed to break me down

I have not slept for over 48 hours

My only mistake is to be a British national with Pakistani heritage

I do not think you will let us leave here

You want to kill us then make it look like accident

What do you want?

Do you want a false confession?

Do you want me to confess to a crime I did not commit?

I folded the piece of paper up into a small square and inserted it into the dish dash I was wearing. If I got back to my cell I would insert it into my shoes and maybe they would throw them out and somebody would find the note. Maybe they would be able to get it into the right hands and prove my innocence. Too many maybes.

With the second piece of paper in front of me, I thought long and hard about what I was about to write. With my head clear, I began...

I am the London bomber

I know all the guys involved who carried out the bombing

I went to school with them

I took them to WHS Smith's where we bought the maps for the underground

I tell them which way to travel

The door opened, Gollum sat down quietly and watched me write. I paused for a second, to think about my next line and Gollum seized his moment.

"We want to know everything about how you raise the money."

I didn't answer him. I was busy writing my confession.

I met with them at the kebab shop and we planned everything.

I got the information on how to make the bomb from hizbollah.com

I went to Argos and B&Q to buy the products needed to make the bomb

I raised the money with a sponsored bike ride and a tombola.

Saddam Hussein is my friend and so is Osama bin laden. I speak to them daily on the telephone

Before you decide to hang me or kill me I want to go on the television and say that jihad is coming and England will be destroyed

Then I signed it.

I handed it over to Gollum, who started to read it. His eyes were wide open with astonishment, as he was slowly mouthing out each word. He stopped suddenly.

"What is tombola?"

"This is a special event that terrorists use to raise money in England. When you tell the British you have me and that I use tombola to raise money, then straight away they will know I am the one; the mastermind." It took all my strength to stop myself laughing.

Hmmph. He nodded his head and carried on reading. When he finished, he got up without saying a word and left the room, returning after a few minutes.

"You have to put your thumb print under your name, Ok."

"Ok, no problem."

I did as he asked, then off he went again. Once more, he was only gone a short while. I was beginning to think that he liked my company. He was followed by a tall guy, well over 6 feet tall, with very dark skin and built like the proverbial shithouse. I gulped, but stood my ground.

"Is this true ? I am the superior officer in charge"

"Yes. This is true."

"Are you sure? Alam, this is very serious. I will take this to the judge in the morning and you will hang."

My heart nearly stopped beating. My stomach tightened and I thought my bowels would release right there and then. I had just signed and thumb-printed my own death warrant. This wasn't what I had in mind when I started to write it. The plan was for them to present it to the Embassy, so at least someone in a position of authority would laugh at the nonsense I'd written and tell them to get my arse out of there.

Brick shithouse spoke.

"Do you want to die? I do not believe this."

"You do not believe this, but you do not believe that I am innocent, so which other thing do you want to believe?"

"I think you are lying."

"I am not lying. Your machine told you I was lying and now I am telling the truth and you do not believe me. Maybe you are lying. I can't win."

"Will you take another test?"

"What is the point of having one more test? You do not believe the first result, why will you believe the second?"

His face couldn't hide the frustration, so he stormed off, slamming the door so hard I thought he'd broken it. Gollum sat down in the big chair opposite me.

"Alam are you really the man?"

"Are you scared now that you know?"

I studied his face as he sat here staring at the floor, seemingly unable to wipe the frightened look from his face. The long silence was broken by a knock on the door. Gollum walked over and exchanged a few words with whoever was there. He looked back at me and with a shake of the head he closed the door behind him, leaving me to ponder on whether I had made a serious miscalculation. I let out a big sigh. I didn't have to wait too long to find out how the statement had been received. A guard came in with a hood and cuffs and walked me outside to a waiting car. I could just about see out of the bottom of the hood, so looking down at my feet I could see it was dark already. Later than I thought, so they must have been messing with my food times to muck up my perception of time. The car took me to the other building, where I was led through all the usual doors and gates and placed into a new cell. More than anything, I was just happy they had chosen a cell that was clean and bright, with air conditioning that worked. Not only that, the AC was at a comfortable level and the TV only flickered occasionally.

I sat down, surprised that the guy left the door slightly ajar. He soon returned, bringing with him a food box. I was so hungry that I ate the lot. The wilted salad and dishwater soup barely touched the sides. Taking the folded piece of paper out of my pocket, I lifted the insole of my shoe and placed it underneath. I curled up and tried to sleep. I was left alone in my cell, nobody came to the door and nobody spoke over the intercom. At first, my sleep was very disturbed, with the most vivid dreams and nightmares intertwining along with the sound of a guy screaming and begging for mercy. It took me a while to realise that the screams were not in my head; they were from a cell two or three doors down from mine. His screams and cries reverberated around the walls; they must have been beating him non-stop for hours. Every now and again I heard footsteps come close to my cell door and figured I was next in line. At some point I became oblivious to the cries for mercy and managed to sleep. The exhaustion had finally caught up with me properly. Maybe it was a combination of writing out the false confession and the truthful note that was now hidden in my shoe. Maybe I had emptied myself of all the frustrations and anger that had been bottled up for days and my mind could finally rest. I don't know how long I was left alone, or how much real sleep I had, but I remember opening my eyes and seeing daylight filtering through the tiny window high up on the wall.

Morning

Sunlight streamed in through the letterbox window. I lay on my back watching the dust particles dancing in the laser beams of light. I heard doors opening and then slamming shut. The morning prayers came over the loud speakers. The jangle of the keys came closer to my door; along with the swish swoosh of the flip flops. When my door was opened, the guard popped his head in and handed me my breakfast food box.

The guard was smiling, which unnerved me somewhat. Oh lovely. The usual fare of processed cheese and slice of bread, along with a carton of juice. I ate all the food, knowing that today might be an important day, so I needed all the strength I could muster. I told myself that taste didn't come into it, this was just fuel. I sat there for a while just going through the previous day in my head, then I had a little walk around the very limited space. I knocked out a few press-ups and sit ups, but they tired me out, so I lay down and tried to sleep again.

Chapter 11
Hangman

I lay there with my eyes closed. Sleep may not have been possible, but it was a relief just to rest my eyes. Well, morning had come and nobody had turned up to ask me about my last meal before I was to be hung. I thought about what I would choose and then thought that I wouldn't eat anything. As I mulled this over, I finally decided that I would ask for loads of different foods and stuff myself silly, so that when they did hang me, I would shit myself good and proper and they would have a right mess to clear up. I laughed at the thought of it, picturing myself hanging there with shit literally pouring out of me and frantic guards getting covered in it as they struggled to get me down. I must have drifted off to sleep, as I was woken up with a start by the slamming of doors. I looked up and saw a face standing over me.

"Get up quickly. Take your clothes."

He pointed to a pile of clothes on the floor, which I realised were my jeans and my Jordan 23 t-shirt.

"Come, come quickly."

I grabbed my clothes and my guard hurried me out of the cell, down the corridor and into the showers. No cuffs or blindfold this time.

"Quick, quick, shower."

I showered as quickly as I could. The guard was

continually pointing and harrying me, so I didn't have a chance to get my thoughts together properly. Was this it? Am I going to court, or will they just hang me now and say I was tried and convicted and they have the confession to back it up?

As I stepped out of the shower he pointed, "Put on clothes. Come on, quick."

I dressed hurriedly; my guard grabbed my arm and pushed me out the shower block as I was still doing up my jeans. He led me further down the corridor where another guard stood by a big metal door. The two men nodded to each other, the door was opened and I was led through it, into a courtyard.

"Wait here, Ok."

I stood there looking up at the sky. It was amazing; so blue and so clear, no clouds to be seen anywhere. I saw a bird fly past and thought this is the last bird I will ever see. I took a deep breath then looked around me. I was enclosed by four walls, with a row of letterbox windows high up all the way around. So there must be cells on all four sides, I thought. That's a lot of prisoners being interrogated. In the corner was a multi-gym gathering dust and a few filthy mattresses which looked like they were ready to be thrown away. Either that or they were being moved to the other building, where I had been on a mattress in a worse state than some of these ones. I walked around the courtyard and came to some potted plants. I touched the leaves and smelt the flowers. How much do we take life for granted? How much do we ignore the little things around us that should be appreciated? Tears filled my eyes and I gave my thanks to god for giving me time on this earth. I told him that I appreciated the beautiful things he had gifted us. The door opened slightly and a very skinny dark man popped his head round. He smiled a friendly smile then came into the courtyard. He beckoned me over to something with a canvas cover. He pulled the cover off to reveal an old barber's chair and gestured for me to sit down in it. I did as he asked, he wrapped a hot towel around my neck, then gave me a shave with a slightly blunt razor. My stubble had grown out of the designer look I'd sported when I was first arrested, into something very thick and messy. With my beard sorted out, he whipped out a pair of clippers and gave my hair a quick trim. All the time he never spoke a single word; he just went about his job with a big grin on his face. I figured he was probably a Bangladeshi, or maybe a Sri Lankan. He had that look about him, with his jet-black hair, dark skin and friendly demeanour. When he was done, he nodded to me, then went and knocked on the door. The door opened and he was let back inside. Instead of closing the door again, the guard came over to me with a blindfold and cuffs. I guessed I wasn't going back to my cell, if these were going on. He took me through another gate on the far wall and we were outside. He guided me into a car and this time I was put in a sitting position, which made a nice change from being forced to lie down, or being sat on the floor. I realised I was sat next to somebody, my blindfold allowed a little peek down to my left and I could make out a pair of shoes that I recognised. Oh my god, I was sat next to Z! I wanted to say 'hi buddy' but thought better of it. I took it to be a good sign that we were together. It was me who had written the false confession; I had not implicated my friends in any way, so if we were all being taken somewhere together, maybe it was to see someone in authority who would see through the bullshit and set us free. The car came to a stop and I was led up some stairs and into a cool room. My blindfold and cuffs were removed and I was told to sit down and wait quietly. I looked around...this is it... this must be the judge's chambers or something. I thought about the outcome; either death or a lifetime in jail, with Moonface for company. Whatever the outcome, I was prepared. I looked at my hands and realised they were shaking. My heart was beating so fast and loud, pumping the blood with such a force it was giving me a headache. I sat and waited for what seemed an eternity, when the door opened very slowly. I gulped, took a deep breath and held it. I was shocked when an Asian woman entered. She told me her name was Rehana and that she was from the British Consulate here in Dubai.

I cannot begin to describe the relief I felt right then. I let out an audible sigh and then burst into tears. I told her what they had accused me of and expressed my complete innocence. I told her how they insisted that I had some connection with the London bombings, how they had constantly threatened us with death or a lifetimes imprisonment, how they had deprived us of sleep and finally how they had steered me into writing a false confession. Looking visibly shaken, she reassured me that there had been a misunderstanding and that all efforts were being made to get us out of there as soon as possible. She told me that the Embassy had only been informed of our detention two days earlier and had asked to see us immediately, but the request had been denied by the Security Services. I told her we were being interrogated around the clock, had endured beatings and sleep deprivation and that only this morning I had been allowed a shower and shave, so that I would look presentable for this meeting. Rehana told me that the Dubai authorities wanted to deport us and the cheeky bastards had told her we needed to provide our own tickets out of there. She told me that she was still concerned for our well-being and emphasised the point that we needed to be out of the country immediately, as it was too dangerous for us to stay there. She was hopeful that we would be released the following morning, which was a Sunday, she told me. If not the morning, then the afternoon at the latest. There was a knock at the door and an older English lady popped her head in.

"Rehana, I think we have a little mix up. I have Mr Z in the other room; you wanted to speak to him? Is this Mr Alam?"

Rehana left the room, telling me on the way out not to worry, it is nearly over.

Christine introduced herself and then knocked the wind completely out of my sails. She handed me a leaflet regarding the services the consulate offers and a list of Dubai based lawyers. She told me that the consulate could not and would not interfere in matters of this kind. I went into shock and told her that Rehana has just explained steps are being taken to get us out of here and you come in and tell me basically that I'm screwed and better get myself a lawyer. What is going on?

Where Rehana had given me hope, this bitch had totally taken it away. Christine must have sensed my anger and frustration boiling over, as her face softened into a smile and she told me that my family had been informed immediately, everyone was in good health and my sister had asked her to convey a message that they all missed me and that my mother was fine. She produced a letter that had been faxed over from my girlfriend. I broke down again as I read it. It was uplifting and positive, explaining everything that could be done was being done to get us home. I guess my time was up then. Christine said she had to speak to the others and wished me good luck. She gave me a hug, which I really needed and then she left.

Shortly afterwards the guard came for me. The blindfold went on along with the cuffs and in the car I was seated next to Z again. We were driven back to the interrogation centre and as soon as I got into the cell the guard told me to get out of my own clothes and gave me a pair of pyjamas about five sizes too big. Miracle of miracles, he gave me a new set of underwear consisting of briefs and a vest. Tearing open the plastic packaging, I changed into them and sat down to watch the telly. My mind was fast forwarding to tomorrow and wondering if it was really true that they were going to release us. I wanted to believe it. I had to.

After lunch had been delivered I decided to have a snooze. I hadn't eaten much for days and was still feeling tired despite a relatively good sleep the previous night. I just wanted the next twenty four hours to be up. I fell into a deep sleep, thankfully no nightmares this time. But still I heard the key turn in the lock and sat bolt upright immediately. The guard told me to get dressed, I was leaving. I have never changed my clothing so fast in my life. I remember a silly thought went through my head that I must have looked like I was Mr Ben in the old cartoon series. He would go into a changing room and immediately change into a new set of clothes.

The guard told me to bring the empty food box out with me. I came out of my cell and we turned right, walking down the corridor. We came to the toilets and he told me to go and throw the box into the large dustbin over by the showers. I did as I was told and as I turned around I came face to face with Raf. We hugged and both of us cried. I asked if he was Ok, he asked me if I was Ok and then the guard shouted.

"No talking!"

We couldn't help but smile at each other.

"Fuck him," I said and we hugged again.

We walked out through some double gates and entered a small lobby area I hadn't seen before. And there was Z waiting for us. We embraced each other and smiled and cried; it was so good to see my friends faces at last. Everybody was asking everybody else if they were Ok. As we all hugged and cried, a door opened and in came Faz. Poor Faz looked to be the most affected by our ordeal. He looked as if he had aged a year for every day that we had been in there. He looked shell shocked and mumbled his words. The poor guy looked like he had been totally broken.

We all went over to hug him, but got little response back. His head hung down and didn't look up once. There were three guards present; one I was familiar with, the others I had not seen before. They were smiling at us, the fuckers. Were they smiling at our happiness? Or at the state of my friend? We sat and waited in silence, until eventually a guy called Ahmed came to speak to us. He took us all into a small side office and explained that they were holding our passports and they would not release them until we had plane tickets in our possession. He made it clear we had to leave their country as soon as possible and that he would ring us and be checking up on us.

We were taken outside to a Land Cruiser and we all

piled inside. As we drove off, we got our first proper view of where we had been held. I looked around and there were armed Police every few yards. The place was fortified by another wall that had guards posted along the top. If I had ever gone through with my plan to make a run for it, I wouldn't have got very far. Nobody spoke in the car; I think we were all just shocked that we were leaving. We left the compound and turned left. The short journey is still a blur and before I knew it, the car had stopped outside the main Dubai Police Station. We got out and just stood there, unsure what to do next. Ahmed got out of the front seat and told us to just go back to the apartment and start organising our flights. He emphasised the point that we needed tickets in our possession before our passports were to be released back to us. With that, he got back in the car and off it sped.

Faz went off to get his car, without offering us a lift or even saying goodbye. The three of us walked along the main road just breathing in the fresh air, with stupid grins on our faces. Every now and then we would just look at each other and burst out laughing. Not that what had happened to us was funny; it was just a joyful feeling to be free again. We had been given our mobiles. Thankfully they must have been turned off during our detainment, as when we fired them up, they still had a charge. First things first, we all made calls to our loved ones, letting them know that the nightmare was over.

Z made a call to Naj, who told us to wait where we were and that he was on his way to pick us up. Standing on the corner of a major intersection, we watched the hectic traffic pass by. I think the initial adrenaline surge had subsided and now we were experiencing the come down. Few words were exchanged, until eventually Naj turned up, along with a friend in another car. Z got into the first car with Naj, myself and Raf jumped into the second. Mr X introduced himself, saying he was a long-time friend of Naj. He was watching the cars go by and pointed out several that he said were secret service guys. They were driving round watching us and had probably been doing so since we were released. He reckoned they would follow us all day long until we left the country.

Arriving at Z's apartment, we sat down and started to discuss what had happened; the threats made, the accusations etc. We all had similar stories, with the same characters saying the same things. On the ride back, Mr X had told us that the apartment was bugged, so we should be careful what we say. He explained that he had contacts in various Police and CID departments and he had been given information that the apartment was supposed to have had drugs planted inside. A raid would be made later that night and by stitching us up and making us look like criminals, the Police would save face.

None of us liked the sound of this, so as soon as we had talked over our experiences, we made phone calls to find out when the next available flight to London was. The first flight with free seats was the following afternoon at 4 p.m., we could go on standby for the 2.30 as well but we had to go and buy the tickets that evening. None of us felt safe in the apartment. We sat around watched TV and then tried to sleep a little, but nobody could relax. There was only one solution and that was to get out of there and stay in very public places where hopefully any 'accident' would be witnessed by too many people, making it impossible for the authorities to cover it up.

Z's phone rang; it was Ahmed. He wanted to know where we were, what we were doing and when would we go to buy the tickets. Z told him we were going to pick them up in an hour. We left the apartment and went to our favourite the KFC restaurant at Karama on the way to the ticket office. Fried chicken had never tasted so good. We arrived at the ticket place and booked the flights home. Fortunately there were still seats available on the afternoon flight. Just as we left the centre Z's phone rang and it was Ahmed again. He asked where we were and if we had managed to buy our departure tickets. We told him it was all taken care of, that the flight was for 2.30 the next day. Ahmed told Z he would ring him in the morning and arrange for somebody to meet us, to give us our passports. We had just stepped outside the ticket centre and were walking towards the car when we saw the 4x4 cruise past us. X had told us what to look out for and we were certain this was a secret service car.

There was one last thing we wanted to do before we left. When we had phoned home, we had learned that some of our friends had come over to look for us. We had told them previously that Seashells and Dawaat were usual hang-outs of ours, so they had gone there and asked about us. The staff and management had told our friends that they had not seen us, when we were clearly abducted from right under their noses. This had pissed us off no end, so we decided we would pay a little visit. When we got there, it was a little early in the evening for things to be really flowing, so the place was pretty empty. We walked through the main doors into the foyer, but there were none of the usual people around. We stepped into Dawaat and saw that all the management were sat at a table, enjoying the entertainment. As it slowly dawned upon them that we had turned up, we saw the whispered conversations and the looks in our direction. Even the waiters looked shocked and none approached us at first. We found our own table and sat down. One of the main guys came over and said hello and asked where we had been. The look we gave him should have killed him on the spot, the cheeky bastard. I grabbed his hand and pulled him in close

"Why didn't any of you bastards tell our friends what happened to us?"

"Oh I don't know anything, sir. I didn't see anything" his head nodded from side to side, his face contorted with fear his body rigid like a board

"I suggest you change those fucking glasses then. Send over a waiter for our order," I said, as menacingly as I could. The man scurried off quickly, clicking and pointing to a waiter who hurried over to us.

We ordered the usual; one red bull for Z, pot of tea for Raf and a bottle of water for me. I figure it shouldn't have come as a surprise that we couldn't relax in there. Every time the door opened our heads would turn simultaneously. If anybody came in wearing a dish dash, we automatically assumed they must be CID or secret service people. We lasted about an hour in there before we decided to go for one last drive around Dubai. We were almost certain that we were being followed; I kept an eye on the cars that were around us, looking for any that reappeared at intervals. We kept on the move all night, until eventually we drove up to Jumeira Beach just as morning was breaking. We sat and watched daybreak, no one uttering a word. I think we all knew that we wouldn't be returning to Dubai, so what better view to have as a reminder. Something beautiful to counteract the pain of our other memories. We waited until the sun had cleared the horizon, then we headed back to the apartment to get ourselves ready for our flight.

Chapter 12
You Can't Leave

It must have been around ten in the morning that Ahmed rang. He gave instructions that we were to go the main Police Station and wait in the car park, where somebody would come and meet us. I convinced the guys that we should take our luggage with us, as we may have to just make a dash for the airport. We set off early and pulling up into the car park, we looked for a spot that would be facing the main road. We wanted passing cars to be able to see us, as well as people passing by on foot. We did not want to take any chances whatsoever and none of us would relax our guard until we arrived back in England. We waited and waited, so many cars went by, but none stopped. The phone rang and it was Ahmed. He apologised and said he was running late, but he wouldn't be long, so we should still wait there.

I didn't like the sound of this at all. I checked my watch and saw that we had already been waiting an hour longer than he had said. We waited another 45 minutes until he finally showed up. Winding down the blacked out window, he looked all of us up and down. He motioned Z to step forward and whispered something to him. Z turned around and told me and Raf that Ahmed wanted someone to get into the car and go with him. Z walked round to the passenger side of the van and got in.

I didn't like this one bit. I didn't trust Ahmed and couldn't see any reason why he couldn't just hand over the passports as promised. We stood there in the blazing sun, watching the minutes tick by. I nipped into the Police Station and bought a couple of cokes from the vending machine. I got back to the car and Raf said that Z had just rung him and said somebody was coming to pick us both up and not to worry. I thought they might be stitching us up, but didn't want to say. I saw the unease I was feeling on Raf's face too. The 4x4 pulled up and we were beckoned to get in. I soon recognised the walls of the compound where we had been held. Driving across the rough ground of the car park, I felt every bump just as I used to when I had the blindfold on. But this time I could see the armed guards and double set of large walls that encircled the place. We pulled up outside some offices and were led to some sliding doors. They whooshed open and I realised it was the place I called sleep deprivation central.

We walked in and sat behind a desk was Gollum, Fatty and the angry man who told me I was to be hung in the morning. They all spoke in a cheery manner which made my stomach turn. I could beat these bastards to death with my bare fists for the shit they had put me through. We were given our passports, our laptops and any other things they had taken from the apartment. Z had a load of business files and paperwork to take back, so we loaded everything into Ahmed's vehicle, taking a couple of trips each. Just as we were leaving, Gollum turned to Z and said,

"Your friend Alam, he is crazy! He so crazy"

Time was running out. We got Ahmed to drop us back

at our car. We quickly transferred everything out of one car and into the other, then sped straight to the airport. We had to be at the airport in less than an hour, so the panic was setting in. Z rang Naj and explained our dilemma and told him to arrange for somebody to pick the car up from the airport and we would leave the keys in the rear wheel arch. We made it to the airport, our luggage was checked through and we proceeded to the passport control. Z was cleared straight away and he stood and waited for us. Raf handed his passport to the guy; he thumbed through it slowly, then thumbed his way back. He kept on looking through it, so we asked him what the problem was. Myself and Raf had applied for residency visas the day before we had been picked up and because the visa had not been validated, we could not go through. He told us to wait and got on the radio asking for help. Z's phone rang and it was Ahmed wanting to know if we were at the boarding gates yet. I asked Z to pass me the phone.

"They won't let us through because our visas are not validated. Can you tell them we want to get on the plane and get out of here?"

"This is not something I can help with. You will have to validate the visa before you leave."

He cut the connection. Bastard. Airport officials came and asked us to accompany them to the office. Z came back through the gate, sensing that something was wrong. I was starting to panic.

"Screw this. What is up with these bastards? I am not staying another minute; they have set this all up. They want to kill us. Can't you see that? I do not want to stay another second in this shithole!"

Both Raf and Z tried to calm me down.

"No I won't calm down. Tell them I will fuck up their

plane if they don't let me go. I want to leave right now. Phone the consulate and tell them we need to leave."

Z rang Rehana at the consulate and explained what had happened. I grabbed the phone off him and started shouting down the phone. She tried to calm me down, but I was having none of it.

"Please, tell them we have to leave. They have been following us all night. If we stay here another day they will kill us for sure."

"Please Alam, you must calm down. If you are swearing and shouting they will arrest you at the airport. Please, there is nothing we can do; you have to validate the visa."

The officials explained that we needed to go back to Ajman in the morning and have our visa's validated or we could withdraw the visa application. Until it was done one way or the other, we could not leave. I couldn't believe it. We made our way to the check in desk and asked for our luggage to be taken off the flight. Next we phoned Naj and told him not to worry about the car, as we needed it for one more day.

We told Z to go on without us, but he was having none of it. Together we made our way to the ticket counter and managed to get our flight changed to the following afternoon. Back in the apartment we sat down and planned how we would handle everything. Most importantly, we would have to be in Ajman for 8.00 in the morning so that we could be first in line to sort out the visa application. We tried to get some sleep but none of us could relax. The phone went off; it was fucking Ahmed again.

"What are you doing?"

"We have to go to Ajman in the morning and fix this

visa issue."

"Ok, call me when you are going to the airport."

As soon as darkness fell we got out of the apartment. We grabbed a bite at Ravi's restaurant, then we drove around, playing spot the Secret Service car. Constantly moving and watching our backs, we stuck to the main roads and well lit well-populated areas. It was in the back of our minds that anything could happen and be made to look like an accident. They could bump us off the road, shoot us dead and then set fire to the car. Nobody was going to ask questions here.

In the early hours we received a call from the airport, saying that our luggage had been processed and was now available for collection. When we got there nobody knew where it was and we had a two hour wait as one man after another went off to look for it. Eventually it was brought to us. By the time we got back to the apartment, we decided we might as well set off to Ajman straight away. Better to be too early, than too late.

Arriving at the business centre an hour early, we sat outside in the car park and waited for it to open. We watched the staff turn up and go inside and as soon as a guy flipped the sign on the door, we were inside and ready to set about getting our visa situation sorted out. The man assigned to help us was a really nice guy called Jihad, of all things. We smiled at each other when we noticed the name plate on his desk. It seemed beyond ironic. We explained our problem and told him that we needed this to be done today, preferably this morning, as we had a flight to catch. He suggested that both accepting and cancelling the visa should be done, because one process would be faster than the other but he didn't know which one. He also told us that the normal timescale for this kind of thing was anything up to four weeks. We were astounded. Four weeks! We barely have four hours to sort this out!

"Jihad, you have to help us, we need to leave today, my friend. Anything that you can do, please do it." Z pleaded.

Jihad must have sensed the desperation on our faces, as he opened his drawer and took out a large folder.

"Ok, here's what I can do. I will give you list of all the people you must speak to. I can get you all the forms that they will need to sign and if you can get to see everybody today, then Inshallah, it will happen for you."

"Thank you, Jihad. You are a good man."

We ran between the various departments, asking the officials on our list to sign the forms that Jihad had kindly sorted out for us. We managed to see everyone up to a point, but as we hit the bottom of the list, we were told that this was a high up Consular Official and we had to go to another department that was in a building further up the road. We literally sprinted to the other building, but to our horror the guy we needed to see had just gone for breakfast. Bloody hell, he must have been at work for an hour at the most and already had buggered off to breakfast.

We sat and waited for his return, trying to be positive, not wanting to contemplate for a second that we wouldn't succeed in today's task. The official finally sauntered in and after a few painful minutes where we could see him sitting at his desk looking through the newspaper, the intercom buzzed and his secretary said we could see him now. The man had a few questions and insisted on going through the process one at a time, rather than together; but eventually he took some photocopies, signed the papers and sent us back to Jihad.

Jihad looked through our signed papers, put them in a certain order and smiled.

"You have done very well, my friends. Now I will take these to the various people who need to see them and hopefully we can set up the interviews for this afternoon."

"Interviews? We have to leave this afternoon, Jihad. Please, I cannot stress how important it is that we get this sorted out quickly."

I'll give Jihad his due. He went off for ten minutes or so and when he came back, he ushered us towards a nearby desk and said that he had spoken to a few of the people in the chain and we could see them one after the other. There were a couple of guys unavailable just now, but he had spoken to their secretaries and they would buzz him when their boss returned. It was as much as he could do right now and Inshallah, they would return soon and agree to see us on short notice. We spent a painful couple of hours going over the same questions with one guy after another. Even when you are sat at somebody's desk, other people will come up and hand papers over for signatures, or just butt in and start talking about anything. Colleagues who have nothing to do will wander over and put them off and the chai wallah is constantly asking if tea is needed, or water or coffee. But we kept our cool and one after the other, our list of required signatures got smaller. Jihad came to us a couple of times and gave us a thumbs-up on the officials who had been unavailable earlier, so things were looking possible.

At 1.30 p.m. we got the final signature, Jihad led us to another waiting area, where we were told we would be soon be given the results of our industrious morning. A small, very smartly dressed man came out of the office about fifteen minutes later and gave us each a large A4 sized brown envelope. Me and Raf looked at each other, took a deep breath and tore them open. Un..be..lievable. After all the shit of the last two weeks, we had been granted residency! The phone rang and it was Ahmed wanting to know where we were and how long before we got to the airport. Jeez, the guy must be psychic.

We set off for the airport straight away. I wasn't bothered about the residency either way; I had no intention of ever returning to this place. We got to the airport, checked in again and cleared the passport control with no problems this time. We all hugged with relief and headed off to the boarding gates. We had another hour before boarding, so we wandered around the shopping areas. I decided I wanted a foot massage but the others weren't excited at the idea, so I went off by myself. Raf decided he needed a manicure, so he went off too, leaving Z to sit and wait at the gate.

It felt so good. The girl was pressing hard on the pressure points. I could feel the tension slowly draining out of me. When she finished I went to the manicure counter to see if Raf was still there, but couldn't see him anywhere. I needed the toilet so I nipped into the men's room. I stepped out, shaking my hands dry and my heart almost jumped into my mouth. I thought I was about to have a coronary right there and then. Stood in front of me was Raf, flanked on either side by two men in dish dash's, with the name badges turned around. I could have died.

"Give me your passport."

I was reluctant and asked why? One guy beckoned with his finger tips to hand it over. Looking at Raf, he nodded his head. I handed it over.

"Go back to the gate and wait."

We walked back to the gate, to find Z. We told him what had happened.

"What the fuck do they want now, Alam?"

"I think they want to apologise, so they are going to get us an upgrade to first class." Raf said trying to be positive

"Do you think so?"

"Yeah, what else would they want?"

"These bastards don't want us to leave. I wish I was as confident as you," Z said.

Our gate was opened and people started to board the plane. We sat and waited and I immediately spotted the two men strolling along in our direction. They seemed to be walking extra slowly, as if they were just savouring the power they had over us. The bigger of the two pulled our passports from his pocket and held them out to me. I went to take them, but he held on with a tight grip.

"Make sure you get on the plane," he said, looking at me sternly. And then he let go.

They turned and left. I turned to Z and Raf, fanned out the passports and smiled. We walked over to the gate and handed over our passports and boarding passes. We got through with no problems and five minutes later we were sat on the plane. Still, I couldn't relax properly. Until we were airborne, there was still a chance someone could come and drag us off the plane and into custody again. The plane filled up with the last of the stragglers, the steward closed the door and the Boeing started taxiing to its takeoff position. This was it; we really were on our way home! The plane took off and I fought back tears of joy. I wasn't ashamed in any way at the joy I felt, but I knew I would look a little strange, sitting in my seat and blubbing like a baby. The flight was completely uneventful. Raf and Z both fell asleep almost immediately, but I fought against the exhaustion; I wanted to enjoy these first moments of real freedom. At some point I nodded off and awoke several hours later to hear the Captain announcing that we were starting the descent into London. He said it was wet and cold, so make sure you have your coats handy. I must have been the only one who cheered. The landing was good, as we slowly taxied to our arrival point, I gazed out of the window and smiled at the grey drizzly place I called home. As we disembarked, it dawned on me that maybe we would be picked up for further questioning. After all, it had been stated all along that the government knew why we were there and had given the order to pick us up. Our bags were some of the first on the carousel, we waltzed through customs and immigration and without a second glance we were out into the terminal where friends and family were waiting for us.

Chapter 13
Media Circus

We were home. England. I also noticed the number of armed Police everywhere, especially either side of the barriers as you exit the gates into the main area. I prepared myself, picturing how this was going to go down. The Police would step forward and surround me, Raf and Z. Camera flashes would go off, more Police would rush in and we would be cuffed and escorted off to Scotland Yard for questioning. We exited the doorway and I looked at the Policeman to my right. He stared back at me for a split second and then he looked away. And that was that. We were home. Nobody looked at us twice. Nobody said boo; not a fucking squeak.

We walked over to our friends. We hugged and embraced them and more tears were shed. Bash went off and got the car and soon we were on our way to Huddersfield. I phoned mum, breaking down again on hearing her voice. I told her that everything was ok and I would be home in a few hours. The journey from Heathrow Airport to Huddersfield takes around three hours, but the journey passed in a flash, as we talked non-stop for the entire journey and the time flew by. Bash told us he had been in touch with the Commonwealth Office and the local M.P. as well as the newspaper's and TV people. We had got into Heathrow around ten in the evening, so by the time we got to Huddersfield it was early hours. I went straight home. Vicky opened the door, bursting into tears and squeezing and hugging me tightly. I was so glad to see her but I felt drained and tired. I had intended to go straight to bed, because of the time, but now I was home, I just had to see mum. So after dropping my cases off I drove over to the shop, took a deep breath and knocked on the door. Mum opened it and just lunged at me! We hugged and cried and I didn't think she would ever let go of me again. My brother and sisters all hugged me and cried; the whole family was completely overcome with emotion. Everyone wanted to know all the details, but I told them to wait till the next day. It was late and I was physically and emotionally drained, so I told them I would come by in the morning.

I went back home to Vicky and the first thing I did was take a long hot shower. Standing there under the soothing water, the last two weeks of my life flashed backwards and forwards. I would feel anger and then sadness. Vicky shouted up to me, to see if I was ok, because I had been in there for half an hour. I dried myself off, went downstairs and sat down to watch some television. I didn't say anything and Vicky didn't ask. We went to bed, I curled up in a ball and fell asleep.

I awoke early, feeling somewhat refreshed. My phone had several messages both voice and text. Flicking through the texts I was reminded I had to go and see Bash, Raf and Ziggy at the office. While I was there, we got a call from Sky News saying they wanted to send someone over that morning to interview us about what had happened. We agreed to the interview; I mean, what harm could it do. We had done nothing wrong and if our names had been linked with terrorists, it was only right that we got the opportunity to set things straight. So the people turned up, the cameras were set up and the interview started. Shahid Malik, the M.P. for Dewsbury was there with us, getting his two pence worth in. All day there seemed to be press and TV people coming and going. I took a break in the afternoon and went to see my son. Thankfully he hadn't been affected by what had happened, as Shareen had told him I was away working. I spent all afternoon there, just so happy to spend the time together. There had been times in detention when I thought I would never see him again, so I wanted to savour the precious moments with him. Again, my emotions were too strong to hold back and I found myself filling up with tears again.

More interviews and press followed the next day. Mr Malik appeared to be permanently stuck by my side, milking it for his political purposes. Vicky called me on the mobile; she sounded all stressed about something. Apparently the M.P. for Huddersfield had called on the house phone, wanting to know why she hadn't been contacted about this situation, as I resided in her area. And that really she should have been representing me to the media and would have done a better job. This made me angry. No one seemed to do anything when we needed them the most, but now there was a chance to get their face in the papers, or on the news, the vultures were circling, wanting their little piece of the action. Fifteen minutes of airtime. That was it; enough for one day. I told everyone I wasn't feeling up to any more interviews, I would continue tomorrow. I went home and as soon as I walked through the door, Vicky broke down. One of the neighbours had made a comment to her about my situation. Something to the effect of 'no smoke without fire' and this had really upset her. Also some newspaper or TV crew had rung up and said they were on their way over to the house to interview me. Vicky said she didn't want all this attention and was afraid to step out of the house. Added to this, I couldn't help feeling a touch of paranoia as a Police helicopter seemed to be constantly circling over my house every second of the day.

A few days later it was arranged for me and Raf to go see a psychologist. I told her about the whole episode: how I felt now that I was back home and what thoughts consumed me, now that I was free. I told her that I wasn't sleeping too well and all the other problems I was having, such as being over-emotional. We were both diagnosed with post-traumatic stress and told to contact our respective doctors to arrange some therapy straight away. I decided to help myself as much as I could. I would train every day, eat healthy, pray and meditate. I did my best, but these things don't just disappear overnight. I found some days were worse than others and most nights were broken. The support of friends and family and people who knew me best was what got me through the darkest of days. I would sit outside the shop with mum and I was overwhelmed by how many customers would come and embrace me. I was so touched when many, particularly the more elderly, broke down and said how sorry they were for what I went through. The family had known many of these people for years, so it was heartening when so many said that they knew I was an honest, down to earth guy who no way would be involved in anything. Over the next few weeks I settled back as best as I could.

I spent my time with mum and the family, resting as much as possible. But everywhere I went, I attracted a crowd. Once I was coming out of the mosque on a Friday afternoon and thought I spotted Gollum across the road from me. This happened on a number of occasions and not just Gollum, it could be any of my captors. I would see one of them crossing the road ahead of me or just see their face in a crowd. Every time I imagined this, my anger would flare up and the urge to run up and grab them and probably beat them to death would engulf me. Once or twice I did go up to guys in the street, utterly convinced it was Moonface, or Fatty or whoever.

We decided to take a holiday later that year. Myself, Vicky and the kids took a break in Florida. A few days into a trip, we were at one of the theme parks and I was absolutely convinced that I saw a couple of West Yorkshire Policemen from the C.I.D in the queue behind us. I thought I recognised them as they had trained at the one of the gyms I go to and my friend there had pointed them out to me. After we left the park, I stopped off at a store and bought a brand new pay as you go mobile phone. I called up my sister and told her the new number. I didn't worry her with my bad feeling, I just told her I hadn't packed my charger for my usual phone and so I had bought a cheap pay as you go to tide me over. A few hours later the phone rang and a man started speaking to me in Arabic. I may not speak it, but I sure as hell recognise it. He was talking a hundred miles an hour and I couldn't get a word in edge ways. I thought my sister must have passed on my new number, but who on earth would she give it to that would speak Arabic to me? Eventually I cut him off, telling him it was a wrong number and I didn't understand Arabic. Whether he understood me or not; I'll never know. The next day I had another call. I'm not sure if it was the same guy again, but it was definitely Arabic being spoken. This was starting to freak me out. What were the chances of buying a brand new phone and then within two days having wrong calls, both speaking Arabic? I threw the phone away. My paranoia told me that somebody was trying to stitch me up.

We returned from the holiday and I was more stressed than ever. My sisters started questioning me as to what really happened in Dubai, they were concerned about the different businesses and people that I worked with. Cousins of mine asked why I was picked up and how they didn't understand why the Government would allow this to happen to a citizen abroad..

Over the next year, I spoke to various lawyers in seeking some form of apology and explanation for what we had gone through. This wasn't about monetary compensation, this was about an acknowledgement by the State of Dubai of what had happened and why. We got nowhere fast. Even though the U.A.E is signed up to various treaties and human rights charters, they just don't follow them. You can't take a sovereign state to court; you have to take action against the actual individuals themselves. I had no chance of knowing who they were and no one was going to tell me. Some lawyers told me I would be on a watch list, with my movements and phone calls all being monitored for at least 6 months. Maybe longer. Maybe forever. The stress of it became too much. My relationship didn't hold up to my constant mood swings and general air of anger and frustration, so I moved out from Vicky's and went to live at mums.

Under the freedom of information act, we have the right to access certain files that are held on us. I filled in the application forms and applied for all the notes and files on my case. What I received were papers outlining the conversations between the British consulate in the U.A.E. and the Security people, about gaining access to myself and the others being held. There were large parts that had been blanked out, but by reading the parts before and after, the general gist was that a third party had asked about getting access to us. I have tried to find out who the third party was and hopefully a government inquiry into the detainment and torture of British citizens abroad will shed some light on this. I have never received an apology or an explanation for what took place and why.

POSTSCRIPT

I went over to Bucharest in Romania in December 2005.

A client of mine was looking to open some new offices and expand his software business from central Europe. Our first night was pretty uneventful but our second one made us all very scared. After a fantastic meal we decided to go and check a local bar in downtown somebody had suggested a place that would be busy for a Tuesday. The taxi pulled up and the three of us jumped out as I walked up to the bar a tall well-built guy came out of the doorway looked at me, bowed his head, extended his hand, gave me a brisk shake and moved off closely followed by another guy. Well-built bowed his head shook my hand and moved off followed by another and another and another. There were six guys in total. My friends looked at me.

"Thought you hadn't been here before?"

"I haven't "

I walked into the bar entrance and no sooner had I stepped through the people inside stopped whatever they were doing looked at me and then quickly averted their eyes.

"What the Hell. How come everybody is reacting like this?"

"I have no idea, no idea mate"

I ordered a drink at the bar asked my friends what they wanted and then swung round to be faced by a very attractive tall girl.

She spoke to me in Romanian. I didn't reply just nodded my head and watched her body language and expressions carefully to see if and when she would realise

I wasn't Romanian.

She asked me some questions the inflection in the voice gave the clue. I stared at her and then smiled

"I'm English no Romanian" shaking my head

She stood back, squinted, tilted her head one way then the other and started laughing. Her English was quite good and very clear.

"Oh my god! You're English? How funny." She touched my elbow.

"Why are all the people acting so weird towards me?"

Still laughing "you look like the king of the gypsies...everybody is scared of him. He is very dangerous, that's why nobody will look you in the eye."

My friend overheard the conversation.

"Let's get out of here.fast"

I went over to Canada the following January, a couple of weeks there working with another client. A trip to Venezuela was on the cards. We took a flight over and spent a few days taking care of business and then one day it was decided that I should have some hair extensions put in. Nothing major it was for a dare. They were only a few inches long, to my shoulders in fact. When the time came to leave and I passed through passport control suddenly there was uproar between the people manning the desks. The army came running in, surrounded me, rifles all aimed at me. I couldn't believe it. My friend was on the phone to England instructing his wife call the British Consulate they're taking Al.

His phone was snatched off him and both of us escorted out of the airport to a waiting military vehicle. I refused to get in until somebody explained what was going on.

"Please sir. It is routine please get in the vehicle"

I gingerly climbed in and before long the airport was a distant dot on the horizon. We pulled up outside a large building flanked by guards on every side as we were escorted through the corridors it dawned on me that it was a medical facility.

A doctor pointed to a room and we stepped in. Some more military guys came in and stared at me. Hands poised on revolvers.

"Strip off remove your clothes".

A gown was shoved in my hand. I undressed and pulled the gown on which was two sizes too small my naked butt poking out the back of it.

"Come with me" the doctor beckoned me into another room

"Stand here do not move" My stomach was up against cold steel.

The x-rays were pulled off. They crowded around them, meticulously examining the prints and then looking at me. It was like somebody watching a tennis match. They would look at the picture then at me then the picture then at media was handed my clothes, got dressed and escorted back out of the building with my friend in tow. We got in the truck and were driven off.

Back at the airport we were taken right to the front of passport control the soldiers spoke with the main man pointed at me and waved their hands. He stepped forward

"Sorry Mr Alam my apology. You look like the drugs warlord, we had to be sure. Please enjoy your flight"

With that I was free.

Apart from the crazy incidents above I continued to travel and work.

I did go back to Dubai a couple of times to tie up some loose ends with work. Was I scared? No I haven't done anything wrong so why would I be. Passport control looked at my residence visa and asked me why I had not had it stamped for endorsement. I shook my head and told him I had changed my mind and that there are much better countries around the world to live in and work. His puzzled look was a joy.

I learnt many lessons from the experience. Not judging people too quickly and also paying very close attention to how and what they respond to. I learnt that no matter what the incentive and how you think the grass may be greener on the other side it most always is not. When faced with difficulty we have a choice to make. We can believe the external environment or we can withdraw internally and change the environment within our heads. The many filters we have can be changed by changing our focus. You can choose how you will respond. Life is only a battle if you let it be.

My life experience, education and self learning led me to being able to cope with what happened . Drawing on studies of Human behaviour, Psychology and sociology along with the fortune of working with some truly remarkable people gives me an insight and unique perspective.

I call it the I.N.N.O.C.E.N.T. mindset:-

Influence
Non verbals (body language also known as Kinesics)
Negotiate
Observation
Calibrate
Elicitation
Neutral
Trust

I have been very fortunate to have travelled extensively and worked with many different people from entrepreneurs, C.E.Os. of companies to politicians and in so many industries, financial, property, banking aviation and even ironically as an adviser on an anti-terrorist program. The above framework has been used on many levelsUnderstanding communication and applying body language and principles of influence are skills essential to those that want to do well.

Thing is my work has always come by word of mouth recommendation. People google my name and are fascinated by my experience. They want to hire me knowing that I coped in such an extreme ordeal and that my tough mental attitude will serve them and their business well ,handling negotiations with ease.

I have been fortunate to meet many wonderful people from all walks of life. They have all touched my life in many ways. I hope I have brought some good to theirs.

My mother passed away in June 2009. The depression and grief I suffered was with me for nearly two years. I worked less but could not detach completely and anyway my mum wouldn't have wanted that. My friends rallied round I am eternally grateful for everybody's help. I am left with the unshaken belief that my mother instilled in me. Always be true and truthful to yourself and others. Treat them with kindness and love. You can do and be anything you want never let anybody limit you and most importantly don't limit yourself.

It has taken a number of years for this book to be published. It would have been sooner had the promised inquiry materialised. Lawyers advised me to hold on and not publish anything until after the inquiry had taken place as it would be detrimental to my case.

No apologies or explanations have come forth to this day.

ABOUT THE AUTHOR

Alam Ghafoor lives in Manchester works in the UK and Internationally.

A father and husband, does his best to fulfil both roles. Working as atrusted adviser consultant and coach to senior execs and CEO's.

His forte is negotiations, influence, Body language and business strategy. Working hard to build a legacy which he plans while walking his dog in the hills.

You can learn more about the I.N.N.O.C.E.N.T Framework and how to apply in your organisation or for your own success by contacting me through my website I am available for Speaking ,coaching and consulting.

Follow me on twitter @AlamGhafoor and Facebook.

www.AlamGhafoor.com

APPENDICES

APPENDIX 1

DUBAI: A JEWEL IN THE MIDDLE EAST

Set against the backdrop of sand and sea is a remarkable city. Dubai, once little more than a sleepy backwater town, has sprung out of this desert wilderness in the last thirty or so years to become a modern, cosmopolitan city whose inhabitants have arrived from the four corners of the globe to embrace a liberalism not enjoyed anywhere else in the Middle East. This glittering mirage is home to Arabs, Indians, Filipinos, Iranians, Russians, Europeans and Americans.

- Dubai is one of the seven Emirates of the United Arab Emirates. The others being Abu Dhabi (the capital), Ajman, Fujairah, Ras al Khaimah, Sharjah and Umm al Quamam
- The United Arab Emirates borders Oman and Saudi Arabia.
- It has the largest population with the second largest land territory by area of all the emirates after Abu Dhabi, owed no doubt to the artificial coastlines provided by the palm.
- The earliest mention of Dubai is in 1095 and the earliest settlement known as Dubai town dates from 1799. Dubai was formally established in 1833 by Sheikh Maktoum bin Buti al Maktoum when he persuaded 800 members of the Bani Yas tribe, living in what is now part of Saudi Arabia, to follow him to the Dubai Creek by the Al Abu Falasa clan of Bani Yas. It remained under clan control when the United Kingdom assumed the protection of Dubai in 1892. Its geographical location made it an important trading hub and by the beginning of the 20th century it was an important port.
- In 1966 oil was discovered. Dubai and the emirate of Qatar set up a new monetary unit to replace the Gulf rupee. The oil economy led to a massive influx of foreign workers, quickly expanding the city by 300% and bringing in international oil interests. The modern emirate of Dubai was created after the UK left the area in 1971. At this time Dubai, together with Abu Dhabi and four other emirates, formed the United Arab Emirates. The following year Ras al Khaimah joined the federation while Qatar

and Bahrain chose to remain independent nations. In 1973, the monetary union with Qatar was dissolved and the UAE Dirham introduced throughout the UAE. A free trade zone was built around the Jebel Ali port in 1979, allowing foreign companies unrestricted import of labour and export capital. The Gulf War of 1990 had a negative financial effect on the city as depositors withdrew their money and traders withdrew their trade but subsequently the city recovered in a changing political climate and thrived.

Today, the City of Dubai has emerged as a global city and a business hub. Although Dubai's economy was built on the oil industry the emirate's model of business drives its economy with the effect that its main revenues are now from tourism, real estate and financial services, similar to that of Western countries, although the last two have declined substantially recently (2007 to present).

Around 2004 onwards the hype about Dubai was beginning to build. "Lying on the calm, azure waters of the southern Gulf and flanked by the majestic desert, Dubai offers year-round sunshine and five-star luxury along with the adventure of a unique Arabian experience."

Newspapers were all singing from the same hymn sheet. Travel writers gushing sycophantically about Dubai, Dubai the Las Vegas of the middle east. Dubai the new Disney land. Dubai playground of the rich and famous. What with Glossy brochures raving enthusiastically about this wonderful desert oasis and billboards encouraging Brits to leave dreary weather and come and sample all that it had to offer.

Everybody wanted a piece of Dubai and why not? Within 8 hours or so flying time from the UK you could step into a whole new world of luxury, leave the airport in air conditioned taxis. Every hotel, every building a luxurious decadent piece of architecture and inside would be the crème de la crème of interior design. You could spend your days in shopping malls NOT just any shopping malls but the biggest in the world all filled to the brim with the latest designer brands as well as the Dubai shopping festival (dsf). This annual month long event is usually scheduled during the first quarter of the year. It is the region's largest and longest running shopping and entertainment extravaganza. All price ranges were catered for and considered cheap compared to back home thanks to the tax free economy. Or maybe you could get lost in the maze of souks with silks spices and more gold than you could possibly carry and not a security guard in sight. It really was a case of seeing is believing. There was always something to do, day or night.

Desert Safari - This is a fantastic adventure trip to the Dubai desert. A 4WD vehicle will take you through the golden sandy dunes to a central camp in the middle of the desert. You will then have a barbecue dinner while enjoying the traditional belly dancing performed by young Arabic girls. Liquor is available to buy in this desert camp.
Camel rides and Dune bashing are some of the other activities you can do during the desert safari.

Visit the Dubai Gold Market - This is the only place in the world where you could see tons (yes tons) of gold in jewellery shops without a single security guard. Some necklaces are so big you wonder how a person can wear them comfortably!

Burj Al Arab 7 Star hotel - This is a truly luxury hotel. You cannot just walk in. You need to buy a ticket to go and see the inside of the hotel.

Tip: There are restaurants for the public inside the hotel, for which you need to buy a voucher.

Ski Resort- Dubai has the world's largest artificial Ski resort. It is worth visiting this resort even if you are from the North Pole.

Wild Wadi Water Park - This is a place where both kids and adults can enjoy water rides. There are fantastic adventure rides such as almost a free fall from 25m heights. This theme park is using the latest technologies. You do not have to walk from one ride to another as they are linked to each other. You must visit this place especially if you have kids.

The marketing machine went into overdrive the tallest building in the world Burj Dubai which is now known as Burj Khalifa will be built here.

Armani will build a hotel, followed closely by Versace. You could literally sleep with the fishes in unique underwater hotels and dine in the stars with opulent sky high restaurants. The palm will be a giant man made palm like structure that will jut out into the sea using huge tracts of land reclaimed from the sea itself with hotels and apartments and the colossal Atlantis resort at the end of it. Islands resembling the globe from space. The most exclusive of addresses accessible only by boat or plane. There were cranes everywhere, more cranes than anywhere else in the world. Each building site was crawling with workers in green blue yellow or red working around the clock 24/7 365 days of the year. The stars came flocking buying up plots or even handed them free for the publicity generated. The Beckham's, Rod Stewart, Tiger woods, Shah Rukh Khan, Donald trump and of course the wives and girlfriends of lusty footballers and pop stars came to mend their broken hearts. It was of course the place to be papped!

So as not to feel left out the middle classes could come and be waited upon hand and foot and pretend for a little while that they too were part of the higher echelons. Then, the building frenzy started to build up and the speculation bubble began. People could buy into the dream own an apartment here for 10 per cent down.

Within a month or two at most the price would double for the building and there was nothing to stop you from selling it on. The main five builders were all owned and run by sheikhs tied in with the ruling family. The airport was expanded and new free zones were created specifically for businesses. Brits came in their droves looking for work and the big fat tax free wage packets, it really didn't matter how skilled you were or how talented. As long as you could blag your way in you could have a piece of it.

Dubai land was announced. A bigger and better theme park than Disney world itself. Dubai was bigger and better than anywhere. You couldn't help but believe the hype and once sucked into it, it was hard to see otherwise.

My visits there were enjoyable. We would dine at the best restaurants and stay in the finest of hotels who really knew the meaning of 5 star luxury. Even the 3 star hotels were better than anything back in the

UK and most of the world. The fast and expensive cars would whiz by you all day long. It was the norm here. You would see famous sports people, film stars and bollywood stars regularly and find yourself sitting next to them at a restaurant. Desert safaris on big ugly 4x4's or quad racing in the sand. Jet skiing on the water front it was like living in a movie.

There was always somewhere to go day or night.

APPENDIX 2

London bombings Time line.

LONDON 7TH JULY 2005.

Four suicide bombers struck in central London on Thursday 7 July, killing 52 people and injuring more than 770.

- The co-ordinated attacks hit the transport system as the morning rush hour drew to a close.
- Three bombs went off at or around 0850 BST on underground trains just outside Liverpool Street and Edgware Road stations and on another travelling between King's Cross and Russell Square.
- The final explosion was around an hour later on a double-decker bus in Tavistock Square, not far from King's Cross.

Four bombs:

Three on underground trains

One on bus

Victims:

26 at Russell Square

13 on the bus at Tavistock Place

7 at Aldgate

6 at Edgware Road

Suicide bombers:

Hasib Hussain

Mohammad Sidique Khan

Germaine Lindsay

Shehzad Tanweer

7th JULY 2005

- **08:50**: Initial reports of an incident between Liverpool Street and Aldgate tube stations, either an explosion or a collision between trains. The reports from the two stations were initially thought to relate to two separate incidents
- **08:50**: Explosion on train between King's Cross and Russell Square tube stations. Eyewitnesses report explosion appeared to come from outside the train (this explosion was initially reported to have happened at 08:56).
- **08:50**: Explosion on train at Edgware Road tube station (this explosion was initially reported to have happened at 09:17).
- **09:28**: Tube operator Metronet says the incident was caused by some sort of power surge.
- **09:33**: Reports of an incident at Edgware Road tube station. Reports that passengers on a train hit by an explosion attempted to break windows with umbrellas in order to escape.
- **09:46**: British Transport Police announce there had been more explosions at King's Cross, Old Street, Moorgate and Russell Square.
- **09:47**: Explosion on number 30 bus travelling between Marble Arch and Hackney Wick at Upper Woburn Place/Tavistock Square.
- **09:49**: Entire London Underground system shut down.
- **10:00**: National Grid announces there had been no problem with power surges.
- **10:40**: First report of fatalities, government source speaks of 20 dead.
- **11:08**: Bus services suspended across central London.
- **11:10**: Metropolitan Police Commissioner Sir Ian Blair confirms fears that it is a coordinated terror attack, but appeals for calm, asking people not to travel to London or make unnecessary calls to the emergency services.
- **12:05**: Prime Minister Tony Blair speaks out on the incident, calling the attacks a coordinated series of 'barbaric' terrorist attacks.
- **17:30**: Having flown back from Scotland, from the G8 Summit, Prime Minister Tony Blair emerges from a meeting in Downing Street and urges the public not to 'be terrorised'.

- **18:13**: Deputy Assistant Police Commissioner Brian Paddick confirms 37 fatalities: two in the bus explosion at Upper Woburn Place/Tavistock Square, seven at Liverpool Street/Aldgate, seven at Edgware Road and twenty-one in the King's Cross/Russell Square blast, as well as around seven hundred injuries, with roughly three hundred of those being transported by ambulance to London hospitals.
- **21:40**: The Metropolitan Police announce that a person injured in one of the blasts has since died in hospital care.

8 JULY 2005

- **11:00**: Metropolitan Police press conference. Confirmed that there are four blast sites - three on the underground and one on the bus - not six as briefly thought. Gives update on casualties: "The number of deaths stands at more than 50. There were 700 casualties, 350 of whom were treated at the scene, 350 of whom have been treated at hospital. 22 people are in a serious condition in hospital and one person has since died."
- **15:00**: Queen Elizabeth II visits victims of the attacks at the Royal London Hospital and speaks out against terrorism.
- **15:30**: Police Commissioner Ian Blair and Mayor of London Ken Livingstone hold press conference. Confirm total of thirteen people killed in Tavistock Square bomb.

9 JULY 2005

- **12:30**: Press conference given by Metropolitan Police Deputy Assistant Commissioner Brian Paddick, British Transport PoliceDeputy Chief Constable Andy Trotter and London Underground Managing Director Tim O'Toole. Confirmed that the three explosions on the Underground occurred at around 8.50am.
- **19:30**: After a security alert, Police evacuate the City Centre of Birmingham.

12 JULY 2005

- **06:30**: Having identified three suspects from CCTV footage, a missing person's report and documents found in the debris at each bomb site, armed police and army bomb disposal experts conduct three raids in the Beeston and Holbeck areas of Leeds and two in nearby Dewsbury, in West Yorkshire. The Metropolitan Police lead this operation, working in conjunction with West Yorkshire Police.
- **11:30**: Up to 600 residents are evacuated from the area of a sixth raid, in the Burley area of Leeds. Residents are unable to return to their homes for two days following the confirmation that explosives have been found at the site.
- **13:20**: A controlled explosion is carried out at the site of the raid in Burley.
- Luton railways station is closed as police investigate a car parked there and believed to be associated with the suspects caught on CCTV cameras. After a series of controlled explosions the car is taken away for further examination.

13 JULY 2005

- A raid by police and bomb disposal experts takes place at a house in Aylesbury in Buckinghamshire, after the identification of a fourth suspect.
- In response to public pressure, the United States Air Force bases at RAF Lakenheath and RAF Mildenhall in Suffolk lift travel bans imposed on service personnel in the wake of the bombings.

3 AUGUST 2005

- Piccadilly Line returns to service.

Four attempted bombings took place exactly two weeks after the deadly 7 July blasts.

- Once again, they were spread out around the capital and once again there were three on underground trains and one on a bus.
- None of the devices exploded and police recovered a wealth of forensic material.

- Three of the suspected bombers began their journey at Stockwell underground station. Failed devices were found on trains at Oval and Warren Street stations and on a bus in Hackney.
- The fourth suspect entered the underground system at Westbourne Grove. A device was found on the Hammersmith and City line not far away at Shepherd's Bush.
- A fifth device was found in a rucksack abandoned in bushes at Little Wormwood Scrubs two days after the failed attacks.

Four attempted bombings:
- Three on underground trains
- One on bus

Locations:
- Shepherd's Bush station
- Oval station
- Warren Street station
- Bus at Hackney Road

Bomb suspects:
- Ibrahim Muktar Said
- Yassin Hassan Omar
- Hussain Osman
- Ramzi Mohamed

Second explosions

21 JULY 2005

Main article: 21 July 2005 London bombings

- **12:26**: Small explosions occur at Shepherd's Bush tube station (Hammersmith and City Line), Warren Street tube station and Oval tube station.
- **13:30**: A backpack is reported as exploding in east London on the Number 26 bus travelling from Waterloo to Hackney Wick.
- **14:30**: University College Hospital is cordoned off by police, it is feared that the bomber from the Warren Street tube station, opposite, ran into the building.

- **14:45**: Whitehall, which was previously sealed off after the explosions, is reopened.
- **15:25**: A major security alert again closes Whitehall
- **15:30**: A man carrying a backpack is arrested by armed police outside the Ministry of Defence in Whitehall, approximately 20 metres from Downing Street
- **16:00**: Sir Ian Blair now describes the situation as "firmly under control".

22 JULY 2005

- **10:00**: Jean Charles de Menezes is shot dead by plain clothes police at Stockwell tube station.

27 JULY 2005

- **04:30**: Yasin Hassan Omar, suspected of the failed attack at Warren Street on 21 July 2005, along with 3 other men, is arrested in Heybarnes Road, Birmingham. He was carrying a rucksack when he was arrested and, after resisting arrest, was hit with a taser stun gun. Later he is taken to London for questioning by the police.

29 JULY 2005

- **11:30**: Of the other three suspected attempted suicide bombers allegedly linked to the 21 July explosions, two are arrested in London. On that same day, Hussain Osman, the fourth suspect, is arrested in Rome.

The Suspects

Five men accused of plotting to murder passengers on London's transport network on 21 July 2005 are set to face trial in January 2007:

Yassin Hassan Omar, 24

Charged with:

- Attempted murder of passengers on the Transport for London system
- Conspiracy with others unknown to murder passengers on the Transport for London system
- Possession of explosives with intent to endanger life or cause serious injury to property
- Conspiracy with others unknown to cause explosions of a nature likely to endanger life or cause serious injury to property.

Yassin Hassan Omar arrived in Britain from his native Somalia in 1992 aged 11 and was granted exceptional leave to remain in Britain in May 2000.

He lived in a flat with Ibrahim Muktar Said in New Southgate, north London, where he received housing benefit.

Mr Omar is accused of the failed attack on the Victoria Line between Oxford Circus and Warren Street.

He was arrested in Birmingham on 27 July, the first of the five suspects to be held.

Ibrahim Muktar Said, 27

Charged with:

- Attempted murder of passengers on the Transport for London system
- Conspiracy with others unknown to murder passengers on the Transport for London system
- Possession of explosives with intent to endanger life or cause serious injury to property
- Conspiracy with others unknown to cause explosions of a nature likely to endanger life or cause serious injury to property.

Ibrahim Muktar Said is accused of trying to set off a bomb on a number 26 bus in Hackney.

He came to Britain from Eritrea in 1992, aged 14, as a child refugee and went to school in Edgware, north London.

He applied for British citizenship in 2003 and was naturalised in September 2004.

Mr Said was arrested in west London on 29 July, eight days after the attempted bombings.

Ramzi Mohamed, 23

Charged with:

- Attempted murder of passengers on the Transport for London system
- Conspiracy with others unknown to murder passengers on the Transport for London system
- Possession of explosives with intent to endanger life or cause serious injury to property
- Conspiracy with others unknown to cause explosions of a nature likely to endanger life or cause serious injury to property.

Mr Mohamed was arrested in west London on 29 July along with Ibrahim Muktar Said. He is suspected of attempting to bomb the Tube near Oval station.

Hussain Osman, 27

Charged with:

- Attempted murder of passengers on the Transport for London system
- Conspiracy with others to murder passengers on the Transport for London system
- Possession of explosives with intent to endanger life or

cause serious injury to property
- Conspiracy with others to cause explosions of a nature likely to endanger life or cause serious injury to property.

Hussain Osman, also known as Hamdi Issac, was born in Ethiopia but later became a British citizen.

He is suspected of trying to bomb a Hammersmith and City Line train at Shepherd's Bush.

He was arrested in Rome on 29 July, subject to extradition proceedings and flown to London on 22 September where he was arrested by British police and charged.

Manfo Kwaku Asiedu, 32

Charged with:

- Conspiracy with others unknown to murder passengers on the Transport for London system
- Conspiracy with others unknown to cause explosions of a nature likely to endanger life or cause serious injury to property.

Manfo Kwaku Asiedu of Finsbury Park, north London, has been charged over the discovery of an unexploded device found at Little Wormwood Scrubs park in west London.

A sixth man, **Adel Yahya**, 23, been remanded in custody charged with plotting to cause by an explosive substance, explosions of a nature likely to endanger life or cause serious injury to property.

www.NewAgePublishers.co.uk

www.InnocentTerrorist.com

www.AlamGhafoor.com

Lightning Source UK Ltd.
Milton Keynes UK
UKOW03f2209120913

217111UK00018B/1362/P